FOREWORD

A Light on the Seaway is a family story, affection-ately told, with an unusual and romantic setting. Interwoven and intertwined are threads of history of the Welland Canals; their progressions, and their effects on the lives of everyone living in the Niagara area.

Ethel Williamson already has had many articles about the canals, the lighthouse, and ham radio published in newspapers, magazines and books in Canada and England; but this is her first full-length book, in which many surprising and interesting episodes await the reader.

Lily M. Bell, M.A. (Western)

Dedicated to our sons with love.

A Light on the Seaway was written for our grand-children and for all young people who might otherwise never know the special problems and joys of living at a lighthouse.

The Port Weller Lighthouse, as we knew it, will soon become a thing of the past, and it is fitting that some record of its history should be preserved.

I have been encouraged and given helpful criticism by the following, to whom I am exceedingly grateful. John Bassett, Lily M. Bell, Larry Smith and the late Jessie Warren and Thomas R. Merritt.
Also Ron W. Clarke for his editing.

Acknowledgement For Photos

Advance Printing, Cyril E. Williamson, Ontario Paper Co., Ltd., Port Weller Dry Docks Ltd., Scott Misener Steamships Ltd., The St. Catharines Standard and the late Thomas R. Merritt.

CONTENTS

Foreword

The Welland Ship Canal

FOREWORD
THE WELLAND SHIP CANAL

The Welland Ship Canal originated with a waterway, a man, and his dream. The waterway was the Twelve-Mile-Creek, flowing into Lake Ontario; the man was William Hamilton Merritt, and his dream, a waterway for shipping from Montreal to the head of the Great Lakes.

Following the American War of Independence, about 1796, a small group of disbanded soldiers, Butler's Rangers, and a number of American settlers, "Loyalists", trekked to Canada and formed a little hamlet on the banks of a stream called "The Twelve". Among them was Thomas Merritt, his wife and three-year-old son, William Hamilton.

The hamlet became known as Shipman's Corners, later called St. Catharines. It was situated in the Niagara Peninsula, a fertile area, cradled by the Niagara Escarpment, a ridge of land about 400 feet high. Above the Escarpment, and to the south lay another large lake, Lake Erie. The two lakes were joined by the Niagara River, with the mighty Niagara Falls presenting an impassable barrier between them.

The Twelve-Mile-Creek is one of many streams emptying into Lake Ontario, each one given a name designating its distance from the Niagara River. Thus the "Twelve" is twelve miles west of the river, and empties into Lake Ontario at Port Dalhousie. The source is south and west of the town of Thorold, from whence it winds its way through St. Catharines and into the lake.

By the time young Merritt had grown up the Niagara Peninsula had become a thriving and important area.

William Merritt was a slim, dynamic man with prematurely white hair and great ambitions. He and his father owned adjoining farms beside the "Twelve". They built and operated a gristmill and a sawmill as well as running a distillery, a potashery and a blacksmith shop. The mills required water and energy which was furnished by the waters of the "Twelve".

Progress was good until the stream began to run dry. Merritt and the other millers who depended on the water supply became desperate. They built a dam across the waterway to make a reservoir of water which would supply their mills during the dry season, but even this did not meet their needs. They must seek an ample supply of water from other sources.

Merritt knew that four miles to the south, on the Escarpment, above the "Twelve" ran the Welland River which emptied into the Niagara River above the Falls at Chippawa. He reasoned: "Why not channel some of this water into the 'Twelve' by digging a ditch from the Welland River to Thorold and down the Escarpment into the 'Twelve'?" This would assure them of an ample supply of water to run the mills. Further thought indicated if he had to dig a feeder canal for water, he should make it large enough to float barges, which could be towed up the "Twelve" to the foot of the Escarpment. An incline railway could be built to lift the barges over the mountain, permitting them to be towed into the ditch; then to the Welland River and the Niagara River, at Chippawa, and on into Lake Erie.

As part owner of a general store and importing business, Merritt was keenly interested in shipping, for all his goods came by sailboat from Montreal, several hundred miles away. Shipments arrived at his warehouse and store on the "Twelve," where they were sold or bartered for local produce which, in turn, was sent by ship to Montreal or to the area above the Escarpment by cart. The cart shipments had to be unloaded at the dock. It was· the task of unloading and reloading that further strengthened Merritt's desire to build his canal. It would expedite the shipments of goods destined for Lake Erie ports and furnish cheap transportation for his own local products.

Merritt submitted his plan for the waterway to the Government of Upper Canada, which promptly turned it down.

Never one to be easily discouraged, and spurred on by the success of the Erie Canal, recently built between Buffalo, N.Y. and New York City, which was drawing settlers and small manufacturers into New York State, Merritt borrowed enough money to set up his own company, the Welland Canal Company. At the same time he helped establish a local newspaper. This successful venture helped promote the building of the First Welland Canal.

On November 30, 1824, at Allanburg, Ontario, the first sod was turned to begin building the original canal. Instead of using an incline railway to carry ships up and over the Escarpment, it was decided that locks could be built at different levels, like steps. This required forty wooden locks from the lower level to the summit.

Port Dalhousie, on Lake Ontario, was the natural outlet of the Twelve-Mile Creek. This became the entrance to the new canal, which followed the creek from this point through a serpentine valley that twisted and turned through Shipman's Corners. It proceeded to Merritton, and, by cut and lock climbed the escarpment to the summit reach between Thorold and Port Robinson. It then followed the Welland River to the Niagara River, above the Falls, at Chippawa, from whence the ships could sail into Lake Erie.

On Friday, November 27, 1829, after five years of super-human effort, in the face of enormous difficulties, the canal was officially opened. Merritt then boarded the flag-decked schooner, "Ann and Jane," the first vessel ever to sail from Lake Ontario to Lake Erie.

Arriving safely in Buffalo, N.Y., on December 2, 1829, he jubilantly dispatched a messenger on horseback with a letter for his wife, telling of his safe passage and the fulfilment of his dream.

The next day the ship re-entered the canal for its return trip to Lake Ontario; this being achieved safely and with great acclaim. A most formidable obstacle to inter-lake shipping had been overcome; the Niagara Falls had been by-passed. No doubt Merritt's vision of a St. Lawrence Seaway capable of carrying ships from the Atlantic Ocean to the head of the Great Lakes was a very misty one, but this was one giant step towards that goal.

Ultimately the Fourth, and present, Welland Canal was officially opened on August 6, 1932. This canal's alignment is almost exactly north and south, and its entrance on Lake Ontario is the mouth of the Ten-Mile Creek, now Port Weller Harbour. This heralded a new era for inland shipping, and ever since that date the Welland Ship Canal has operated day and night throughout the shipping seasons.

Flight Locks Present Canal
Fourth Welland Canal

Remains of Wooden Locks
First Welland Canal

Abandoned Lock of   Second Welland Canal

Pt. Dalhousie Lock Third Welland Canal

William Hamilton Merritt
Father of the Welland Canal

Opening of

First Welland Canal

November 27, 1829

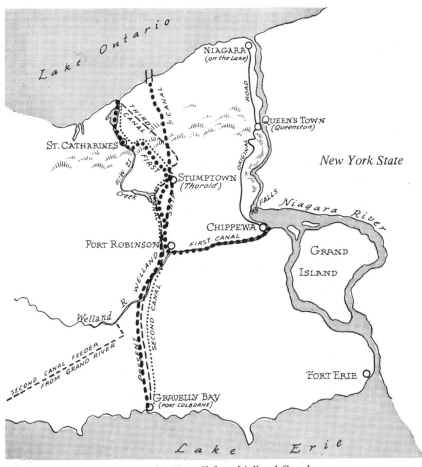

Map showing all four Welland Canals

A LIGHT ON THE SEAWAY
by
Ethel Williamson

Introduction

Early in June, 1969, this message was broadcast to all ships on the St. Lawrence Seaway, - - - "NOTICE TO MARINERS, As of June 23, 1969, the Main Light at Port Weller Lighthouse will be extinguished, and the tower and markings subsequently removed from that location."

The tower and light, a modern Pharos when built in the early 1930 s, must give way to modern range lights and eventual automation of Aids to Navigation on the Seaway.

This news concerned many people in the Niagara area, especially the hundreds of amateur sailors on Lake Ontario who had used this powerful revolving light as a homing beacon for nearly forty years.

Thus, the tower, traditional symbol of lighthouses for hundreds of years, would no longer guide the ships of all nations through the entrance into the Welland Ship Canal; a vital waterway connecting two great lakes of the world-famous St. Lawrence Seaway.

The closing down of the main light tower marked the ending of another chapter of our lives. It has been the focal point of all our activities for nearly twenty-five years.

I couldn't count the times that high tower had played a prominent and often frightening role during those years when my husband, Cy, was the Light-keeper and I, the Light Housekeeper of the Port Weller Light.

It is often said that life begins at "Forty." Well, Cy and I had already lived a pretty full life as we neared that age. It was then we decided to leave the city and move to the lighthouse. We were the most unlikely candidates for the job that one could imagine.

Barely out of our teens, we were married in 1927. Cy was the boy next door. This tall, shy, fair-haired youth had always been my ideal - - - my "Prince Charming."

He worked in an office and I was a hairdresser. We operated a small beauty shop for a short time, then went to Buffalo, N.Y. to make our fortune. We didn't make a fortune but we did make some very good friends. Everything was fine until the Great Depression hit - - - I became pregnant, and Cy lost his job!

Compared to most young couples we were very fortunate. We had a houseful of furniture, a radio and a good used car - - - all paid for! And, most important, I still had my job in one of the smartest beauty salons in Buffalo - - - at least for the next seven months!

Our first son was a beauty, with rosy cheeks and jet black hair. We named him Douglas, for he reminded us of the "Black Douglas" in *Sir Walter Scott's Lady of the Lake.*

Cy couldn't find work anywhere. We cashed in an insurance policy, and he went to barber college. After finishing the course, Cy bought a small barbershop in St. Catharines, including equipment and business. Now, he would be his own boss! It was good to be home again.

Two years later our second son was born. My heart was filled with joy, for he was fair-haired and looked just like his father. We named him Bruce, for "Robert the Bruce."

Fortune smiled on us for we were able to rent a larger house - - - one that had originally belonged to Cy's grandparents, and built by his maternal grandfather. Cy converted two front rooms into a beauty shop for me, and opened a radio and electrical repair shop in the basement. We were busy and happy. I was the love of Cy's life, and I had only one rival - - - Amateur Radio. Our boys were healthy, and a delight to us.

We were busy from early morning until late at night, but the beauty of it was that all our activities were in our own home. Our boys were never neglected for Cy and I were always nearby, to discipline when necessary or to comfort when there was a minor injury. We thought we were the luckiest family on earth.

Cy had built an amateur radio station in part of his workshop, and this was always a place of interest to many young men who shared his hobby, ham radio. Sometimes, after the boys were tucked into bed, and I happened to be through work early in the evening, I felt a little hurt and neglected when Cy was operating his station. If I mentioned this to him, he would say: "don't worry, dear, I'm always right here if you need me."

Sometimes he would say: "y'know, Ethel, this shortwave radio is a wonderful invention. Who knows? One day my hobby may change our lives!"

Little did we know the changes it was to make. The first one came in 1940, when the Canadian Government sent an appeal to all licensed amateur radio operators, to volunteer for service in World War II. Cy felt very deeply about his duty to his country, especially when he knew he was well qualified for the task.

"What would you do in my place?" he asked me one day.

"If I were a man," I said, thoughtfully, yet with fear in my heart, "I would go."

"How will you manage, - - - with the boys and everything?" Cy asked, anxiously. He was well aware of the tremendous changes that would be caused by his absence.

"I'll make out", I assured him. "I'll have to. After all, I have two big boys to help me. We'll be fine honey; just hurry home! " My eyes were blinded by tears.

Cy was commissioned as a Flying Officer in the Royal Canadian Air Force, and five short weeks later sailed overseas on a cruise ship, unescorted, for it was too early in the war for convoys.

After intensive training in Radar, the secret system of detecting enemy aircraft, Cy became the commanding officer of a number of Radar Stations in strategic areas in Europe and the Middle East. He moved around so often, I never knew exactly where he was. Sometimes our letters would take months to reach each other. The years passed by and the waiting seemed endless.

Doug and Bruce were a wonderful comfort to me. I continued with my beauty shop, and became a Red Cross Nurse at the local Blood Donors' Clinic, but in spite of all my activities I was desperately lonely. I suppose my lowest moment came when Cy wrote: "Ethel, it's been such a long time, I hardly remember what you look like! "

Would we ever be close to each other again? We could be like strangers. It was a frightening thought. I'll know right away, I told myself; I know I will!

After more than four years we learned that Cy was coming home. He phoned me from Montreal, and I went to meet his train in Toronto.

The train was delayed for several hours. Union Station was jammed with people, tense with excitement and anxiety. A small band was on hand to greet the servicemen. At last the train arrived! Everyone strained against the ropes, watching for their loved ones. My eyes were dry from the frantic searching of faces as the men marched down the aisle. There were so many of them. Now and then came a scream of recognition. I felt dizzy. I knew Cy would be among the tallest, but there seemed to be so many tall ones.

Suddenly I felt a tap on my shoulder. Snapping my head around and scowling with annoyance at the intrusion, for I mustn't miss a single face, I gazed into the strange, yet oh, such well-remembered deep blue eyes of my husband! My legs turned to rubber. Was I going to faint? No, I mustn't do that. Through tears of joy and relief I saw that Cy was crying too.

How did you find me?" I asked. "I was sure you'd be with the others." Cy led me to a quiet corner of the station.

"When I saw that reception committee waiting, I ducked out another doorway, I just couldn't miss your shining black hair," he whispered, folding me into his arms.

No longer were there any doubts in my mind. Those long lost years melted into yesterday!

Chapter Two

A MOMENTOUS DECISION

One evening in September, 1945, Cy looked up from the evening newspaper. "How would you like to live in a lighthouse?" he asked.

"A lighthouse? Why would I want to live in a lighthouse?" I stopped knitting, and stared at him in amazement. "You must be joking," I said.

Cy knocked the ashes from his pipe and placed it on a tray. "No," he said. "I'm serious. Let's talk about it." He walked across the living room floor and closed the door of the boys' bedroom. "Y'know dear, I'm really worried about the future. If I return to a business of my own as I had before the war, it would cost an awful lot for new equipment and modern tools."

"I'm afraid there's going to be a lot of competition in radio business from now on. So many men received training in radio and electronics during the war, and they'll be looking for that line of work. I've been hoping for some kind of job that I'd enjoy doing, but, after having my own business for so many years, and being a commanding officer in the war, I'd hate to work for someone else." He hesitated for a moment, then pointed to the newspaper. "Here's an ad," he said, "that sounds very interesting. It's for a lightkeeper, on the Welland Ship Canal. The present keeper is retiring at the end of navigation in December. The Department of Transport is looking for a man with experience in radio and electronics, and the position is open for Civil Service examinations." He paused, then added, "I'd like to try for the job."

I couldn't answer right away. The whole idea had come as a shock to me. The past few weeks had brought a number of adjustments in our lives. I had prepared myself for Cy's homecoming with reservations. After all, people can change considerably in a few years. Happily enough, when we met, it was just as if we had never been apart. With the boys, it was bound to be strange. Bruce could hardly remember his dad, but everything had fit into place; even Tippy, the dog we had adopted during Cy's absence, accepted his new master, happily, and Douglas was so proud of his father, it warmed our hearts.

Finally, after a long silence, I said: "But dear, what do you know about a lighthouse? Why, I've never even seen one except in pictures. What about this particular lighthouse? Have you ever been there?"

"No, but I do know something about it. It's located about seven miles from here, at the Lake Ontario entrance to the Welland Ship Canal. It's supposed to be quite modern, with a radio beacon station and all kinds of electrical equipment, all remotely controlled. They need a man who is qualified to operate all the various aids to navigation, and who can make instant repairs when necessary."

4

Cy wasn't joking, I shook my head in disbelief. "Really, dear," I said, "this is an awful decision to make. Why, it would mean changing our whole way of life." I paused, a hundred wild thoughts racing through my mind.

"What about our boys? What about schools? Where would we live?"

"I don't know any of the answers yet, honey, but let's think it over. Y'know, Ethel, this could be the very job I've been looking for."

Maybe Cy was right. We were both nearing our forties; we had two teenage sons to raise and educate, and we longed for a close relationship as a family. During Cy's absence I had become the head of the household, now, it was important that he should resume his former, natural role. If we moved to a new environment, away from all existing influences, we could make a world of our own and recapture those lost years of the war.

The outcome of our discussion was that Cy should send in his application. The more we thought about it, the more appealing it seemed. It promised privacy, security and adventure.

"There's just one thing I must get," said Cy, "and that's a commercial operator's licence. I'll brush up on my Morse code, and write an examination. It shouldn't be too difficult." I could see the old glint of joy in his eyes at the mere mention of radio, his old love.

I still had doubts. It was hard to accept the thought of giving up my comfortable home to live in a lonely lighthouse. "Oh, well," I consoled myself, "maybe I'm worrying needlessly. He could fail the examination." This was wishful thinking.

Cy wrote out the necessary papers and was then given an oral test. "There were eight other applicants," he told me.

We tried to put it from our minds. Then came word that Cy had passed first!

Now, suddenly we were faced with a decision to make. Should Cy accept the job? We still had a choice. The salary was small, but the promise of security; the challenge of new adventures; new fields to conquer, overcame our fears.

The knowledge that Cy would have full responsibility of an important station, as Officer-in-Charge of all aids to navigation was most appealing to him. He decided to accept the position.

Doug, now fifteen, and Bruce, thirteen, had been included in most of our discussions about the lighthouse, but they had little to say. Like all youngsters, they were afraid of any change in their home life. This was the only home they had ever known. It meant everything to them. All their friends lived close by, Doug's High School and Bruce's Public School were both within two blocks of our house, and both sets of grandparents lived within walking distance. We were near the centre of town; thus close by the YMCA, the ballparks, the sports arena and the movie houses.

To move away from all these familiar surroundings to an isolated lighthouse would mean more of a hardship to them, emotionally and physically, than it would be to Cy or me, but they had never rebelled against our plans, and they did trust us. Actually, they refused to believe we were really determined to go until it was an accepted fact. They grumbled at first, and argued against the whole idea, but once they were convinced that their basic home life would not alter they began to show a little enthusiasm, boasting to their friends, who were wide-eyed listeners, of the adventurous lives they would lead at the lighthouse; swimming, hunting and boating. As former Boy Scouts, this was most appealing. Once their pals were convinced, they, themselves, began looking forward to the future. The day Cy's appointment arrived they urged us to visit the lighthouse at once.

"Come on, Dad," they begged. "Drive us down. Oh, Boy! Wait 'til the fellows hear about this!"

Cy had been to see the lighthouse a week or so earlier. The retiring keeper invited him into the Watchroom, where the radio beacon station and foghorn generators were housed. There was a large desk and a panel of impressive-looking switches for the remote operation of lights, foghorn and bell. The keeper told Cy he couldn't show him the living quarters, as someone was asleep back there.

Now that his appointment was official, Cy had misgivings. "I'm afraid you're going to be disappointed," he told us. "It's not at all like you imagine." He turned to me with a downcast look on his face. "Suddenly I feel a bit sick of the whole business," he said. "We know so little about it. All I saw was the Watchroom. How could I insist on seeing the rest of the dwelling when I was not yet sure of getting the job? I'm afraid it's too late now. The lighthouse is closed for the winter, and the keys were sent to the District Marine Agent in Prescott."

"Oh, come on Dad," insisted the boys. "Let's go down anyway. We'd love to see the lighthouse, even if it's only the outside."

Doug and Bruce were still young enough to be full of boyish spirits. Anything that promised adventure and fun was most appealing to them. We donned our heavy coats and hopped into the car, accompanied by our ever-present dog, Tippy.

We began our drive to the lake in high spirits. It was a beautiful scenic ride up Lake Street to the Lakeshore Road where we turned sharply to the right and followed the shoreline towards Port Weller. We had often driven out here before but that had been in the spring time, when the roads were lined with orchards of blossoming fruit trees, and later in the year when there was an abundance of peaches, apples, pears and grapes at farms all along the way.

Somehow, on this cold and bleak day, late in December, everything looked cheerless and depressing.

As we came closer to the Welland Ship Canal we were all silent, each of us filled with uncertainty and fearful of the future. I'm sure we all had the same question on our minds, "What is it like - - - to live in a lighthouse? "

Chapter Three
WE VISIT THE LIGHTHOUSE

"Here's Lock 1," said Cy, as he made a left turn off Lakeshore Road. He parked the car close to the lock wall at our right. "Don't go too close to the edge," he warned, as the boys dashed over to look into the lock. Cy took my arm and we hurried over to join them. We stood for a long time, gazing into that enormous concrete-lined channel. At the northern end of the lock, large steel gates opened wide, and the water in the lock was at lake level.

"Here is where the ships begin their climb up the mountain," Cy explained. "After a ship sails into the lock at lake level, those gates are closed behind it. Water is then sent into the lock through holes on the side walls until the same level is reached as the water above the lock. The upper gates are then opened; the bridge is raised, and the ship sails out of the lock, into the canal, then proceeds to the next level."

"What about ships coming down the canal?" asked Bruce.

"It's the same procedure, only in reverse. The ship sails into the lock at the higher level; the gates are closed behind. Water is drained from the lock and the ship slowly drops to lake level; the northern gates are opened, and the ship leaves the lock. After sailing through the canal harbour, it slips past the pierheads and buoys and into Lake Ontario."

"How big are the locks, Dad?" asked Doug.

"Just a minute. I have the exact figures here in my notebook." He thumbed through the pages. "Here it is," he said. "The concrete walls are 820 feet long, 80 feet wide and 82 feet high. The lift is 46½ feet and the total lift of all eight locks that carry a ship from Lake Ontario to Lake Erie is 326½ feet. The greatest climb is from Port Weller to the summit of the Escarpment at Thorold. That's why they say the ships must climb a mountain."

"How long is the whole canal, Dad?" asked Bruce.

"It's 27 miles long, and it takes a ship about eight hours to sail from one lake to the other."

"I'm dying to see the lighthouse," I said. "Let's go."

Hurriedly, we piled into the car and drove down a short, steep hill to harbour level. Concrete tie-up walls lined the west bank with mooring posts at regular intervals. Here ships could wait their turn to enter Lock 1. Following the west bank, we passed huge mounds of soft coal and lake sand, then drove down a dirt road.

"This is called the West Pier," Cy told us. "The one you see across the canal is the East Pier."

"How did they build these piers?" Doug asked.

7

"Oh, it was a tremendous task. First of all, great concrete cribs, that floated, were made at Port Dalhousie, then towed across the lake to a position about one and a half miles from the mainland, and mouth of the Ten-Mile Creek. These were sunk to the bottom of the lake by letting water inside through valves. These cribs, placed 400 feet apart, were filled with stone, then covered with heavy concrete, to form pierheads for two embankments. A railway trestle was then built from the shore to the pierheads, and it carried flatcars full of rocks and dirt fill, brought from the canal prism, as the excavation was made for the canal bed. This fill became the harbour walls when it had attained a height of between 10 and 16 feet above water level. In the middle, the harbour was deepened to 27 feet. Both piers were identical. It took years to build this harbour, for there were many setbacks; wild storms that washed away the structures; tragic accidents, and a complete stoppage during World War I. There was a terrible shipwreck, just about where we are right now!"

"There are so many trees!" I exclaimed. "How lovely they must be in the summer!"

"These trees were planted for a windbreak, to protect ships in the harbour," said Cy.

Just then we made a turn in the road, and there stood the lighthouse!

"Wow!" cried Bruce. "What a crazy-looking lighthouse!"

Cy stopped the car. We stared in amazement at the towering steel structure that loomed above a square concrete building. What a disappointment! We had pictured a circular white tower, tapering at the top, where a revolving light would throw its beam through little glass windows. Instead, this steel monster, this bridgework, rose some 120 feet into the air like a skyscraper. A square wooden room, perched at the top, had a catwalk all around it. The entrance to the room was a trap door in the floor. Four flights of steel steps with a small platform between each section, led up to the top. One glance at that tower convinced me I'd never have enough courage to climb it.

The keeper's dwelling, standing about 20 feet south of the tower, looked exactly like an army barracks with parapet roof.

"Is this going to be our house?" cried Doug, his face the picture of gloom. All the excitement; all the spirit of adventure had vanished at the first sight of this barren-looking, cold, concrete building.

Cy and I looked at each other and shook our heads. What a bitter letdown. Tippy was the only happy one in the group. He had dashed away through the woods, chasing rabbits!

"Maybe we can peek into the house," I suggested, hopefully. We ran all around to every window but there wasn't a chance. Each one was covered by a dark green blind. By this time we were all shivering, and our teeth chattering from the cold west wind that howled across the lake. We got into the car, and sat there, quietly gazing around.

On this bleak December day everything looked so desolate and forbidding. Huge mounds of earth and rubble lay here and there about the dwelling, exactly as they had been dumped there years ago. A short cement walk led from the road to the front door, facing the canal; another led to a door at the south end of the building. Behind the house, dead weeds, thick as a bush, reached up to the window ledges. Through the woods, about 100 yards to the west was Lake Ontario, reflecting a grey and overcast sky. On our east, just 20 feet from the front of the house was the canal. To the north, and extending another half-mile into the lake, were the two pierheads. Although they were actually 400 feet apart, from that distance, they seemed much closer, like the claws of a giant lobster.

Cy and I sat in silence; each with his own thoughts, but the boys didn't even try to hide their feelings. They grumbled all the way home. Finally, I said, "Never mind, boys, everything will look much nicer in the spring. Just think of all the fun we'll have in the water."

"Can we have a boat, Dad?" asked Doug, his face lighting up at the prospect. "We could practise rowing; maybe become good enough to race in the Henley Regatta, as you did."

"That was a long time ago," said Cy, a smile on his face, "but then, I guess I was about your age, Doug. Yes, we must have a boat. Maybe we could build one. What d'you say to that idea?"

"Oh, Boy! That'd be super!" Doug exclaimed. They both cheered up for a while, but, as they remembered some of the unpleasant things, we could see by the expressions on their faces the future looked mighty bleak to two young lads who had known nothing but city life. Just the thought of riding their bikes seven miles to and from school each weekday was bad enough. Being so far away from town would mean they would have to give up their school sports, baseball games and hockey.

Pt. Weller Lighthouse 1946.

Pt. Dalhousie Light—
Traditional Design.

"What about Sea Cadets, Dad?" Doug asked, anxiously. He was very keen about the group, and had risen to chief petty officer. He often spoke of his hopes of winning a scholarship to Royal Roads Naval Academy. Bruce, too, enjoyed Sea Cadets, but it was mostly for fun, and the cadet band. He played the bugle.

After a few minutes to think it over, Cy said, "It's only on one night a week, Friday; I'm sure you can go."

This news cheered them immeasurably. They began whistling "Anchors Aweigh," and somehow we all felt better.

We were glad to get back home. The boys ran off to tell their friends all about the lighthouse. I thought a hot cup of coffee would help. While we sipped the satisfying brew, Cy looked very thoughtful, then asked, "What d'you think, dear? Have we made a big mistake?"

I didn't answer for a moment, then I said, "It's hard for me to say, Cy. Everything looks so cold and uninviting at this time of year. I'm sure it's quite different in the warm weather. The woods must be lovely, and we could do an awful lot to make the house look nicer."

"It looks like a lot of back-breaking work to me."

"We could all help," I suggested. "I'm sure we'd have lots of spare time to do things. Oh, if only we could see inside the house; I'd be able to measure the windows for curtains, and do lots of things to get ready for the spring. Can't we get the keys, dear?"

"No, honey. I'm afraid we'll have to wait until the Marine Agent brings them from Prescott. It's tough, I know, but we'll just have to be patient."

I felt crestfallen over this news. What a frustrating situation. Here I was, bursting to get busy, with three months to spend on decorating or sewing for our new abode, and my hands were tied. What a predicament!

Later, we discussed all aspects of the job. We knew there would be problems and hardships ahead. So many of the everyday things we had always taken for granted — fresh water — telephone — the corner grocery store — mail delivery, our family and friends who all lived nearby; these we would really miss. On the other hand we must think of the years to come: of raising our sons: the promise of security: and this was a most serious consideration, for we remembered only too well those difficult years of the Depression. We longed for a peaceful life and, hopefully, a close family relationship. These, we agreed would make it all worthwhile, after all.

Well, it was now Christmas time. This would be a real family Christmas; the first one we had had for five years. We decorated the house; had parties for family and close friends, and thanked God for all our blessings.

The holidays passed and we decided to spend the winter remodelling our home. We converted it into three apartments. Two apartments we would rent. This would supplement Cy's salary, and provide a nest-egg for the future. One apartment we must keep vacant for our own use during winter months, for we knew the lighthouse was not adequately heated for year-round occupancy.

The months passed very quickly. We worked hard but it was a joy to be doing things together again. It was really fun, sharing the excitement and fulfillment of building something of our own.

Doug and Bruce seemed to share the urgency of getting things done. They were a great help with the alterations, for there was always a need for extra hands. They also took full advantage of this time to crowd in as many winter sports and school activities as possible.

Cy rented a radio code machine and practised speeding up his code. He then tried an examination and received his Commercial Operator's licence; a requirement for his new position.

By early spring we were ready, for better or worse, to move to the lighthouse, unaware of the trials and adventures that lay ahead.

Chapter Four

LIGHT-HOUSEKEEPING!

The canal was scheduled to open for navigation on April 1, 1946. About ten days before that date an official of the Department of Transport arrived at our house to present Cy with all the keys to the lighthouse and adjacent buildings as well as some books of instructions, on how to operate various aids to navigation at this station.

As soon as he left, Cy and I hopped into the car, and drove to the lighthouse. Cy unbolted the storm door, then unlocked the living room door behind it, and pushed it open.

There, in all its squalor, was revealed our future home!

I took a step backward; shut my eyes, and whispered, "God help us!" I had never seen anything like it in all my life!

I stepped inside, numb with disgust and sick at heart. Gone were any illusions I ever had about romantic living in a lighthouse!

The ceiling of the living room, twelve feet high, was almost hidden by festoons of cobwebs draped like curtains from the tops of the windows to the light fixture, hanging by a chain in the middle of the room. Short curtains that had once been white sheeting, drooped in yellow folds from string ties. When I touched them, they disintegrated in my hands. Dark green blinds had been patched time and time again with wide strips of adhesive tape, at all angles. It looked like a haunted house. Khaki brown paint on the walls had never dried, and everywhere I looked were pictures, cartoons and mottoes, cut from magazines and pasted haphazardly, on the sticky walls, as far as a hand could reach. The floor, once a lovely hard maple, was now a sea of rippling waves caused by years of wet-mopping.

I held back hot tears of disappointment, and bravely faced the other rooms. The bathroom was the worst. Beneath the towel bars lay a mass of dirty lint and fuzz where towels had stuck to the sticky dark green paint. Flies, moths and spiders, long since dead, clung to the walls, along with dozens of mottoes, cartoons, and dust. The toilet sat precariously on a rotting floor, apparently caused by years of water slopped from pails, which had been carried from the canal to flush the toilet. No water ran from the taps in the wash basin or the bath tub. Five pails sat, rusted, in the tub, available for future flushings. A note, pasted on the wall, read, "We don't talk about bathrooms in this house!" No wonder! I thought, closing the door in disgust!

The bedroom and kitchen were on the north side of the house. The bedroom was a fair size, with the same high ceiling as in the rest of the building. It had two narrow windows and a small clothes closet. The painted walls were dingy but not tacky, and nothing was pasted on for decoration, thank goodness! The kitchen — well, that was out of this world! Cy opened the door, and we both took several backward steps, as a horrible stench momentarily overwhelmed us!

"Open the doors," said Cy. "There's something rotten in here. I'll have a look."

I threw the doors wide open, and all the windows, then went back to the kitchen. A large, black hand pump sat on a drain board by a kitchen sink. Cy was pumping for water but none came. He noticed a trap door in the middle of the floor and, on opening it, we found a cistern, half full of black water. The smell was stronger than ever. Cy's flashlight revealed a dead rat that had become caught in the water pipe that fed the pump above! It must have been there all winter.

This reservoir, beneath the kitchen floor, had been built to hold rainwater, that collected on the flat roof, then ran down a drain pipe into the tank below. This, presumably, was our supply of fresh water. Well, whoever had designed that for this particular lighthouse, had no knowledge of the hundreds of ships sailing close by, with their smoke stacks filling the air with black soot, which had settled on the roof these many years!

The only heat in the building came from four old portable heaters. They were rusted, and the electric elements would have to be replaced to be of any use. Imagine this, in a house, a mile and a half into the lake, and so exposed to the extreme cold of a Canadian winter!

It seems that during the war years, everything had been sadly neglected. It had been impossible to get even casual help, and no one had worried about conditions as long as the lighthouse operated on schedule.

If there had been more time before the opening of navigation, we would have given up right then, but — with navigation about ready to start — there was no time to back out; no time for the government to hire another man. We had to face it. Cy 'phoned the head office in Prescott and told them the condition of the place, and that something must be done at once. Luckily, they gave us permission to hire decorators to fix the walls.

Fourteen wooden steps, badly in need of repair, led down the canal bank to the water level of the canal. Cy went down to fill a couple of pails. I heard him call, "Ethel! Guess what? There's a pump! — a water pump!"

"What does that mean?" I asked, running to the top of the steps.

"It means we'll have running water; canal water, if this thing works!" He examined the electric pump carefully. "Looks like it hasn't run in years," he said. "I'll take the motor out and try it."

"Oh, it'd be wonderful to have running water, dear. It seemed strange to have bathroom fixtures and no water."

"Well," said Cy, "I also noticed an electric hot water heater and tank in the little switch room. I knew there must be a pump somewhere. When I saw that wooden box at the foot of the steps, I pried open the lid and there it was."

Cy decided that fixing the pump should be his first job. He stripped the motor, then began re-winding it by hand. This was a long, tedious task, for the wire was fine, and must be wound neatly, for a specified number of turns. Meanwhile, I swept down cobwebs, cleaned out closets and kitchen shelves, tore down the remnants of curtains, and tried to scour stains and rust from the bathroom fixtures. I just knew Cy would make that pump work!

After the motor was wound, it had to be taken to the Crocker Wheeler, and processed in the factory oven. This took two days. During that time we rented a floor sander and smoothed the floors enough to be stained and varnished. Cy repaired the bathroom floor and we laid a light-coloured mastic tile. What an improvement!

We bought venetian blinds for all the windows, after the decorators had sanded and cleaned the walls, and painted them with pastel colours. The transformation was unbelievable.

The Watchroom was the largest room in the house. As there was only one bedroom, we had to find a place for the boys. The Watchroom was our only hope. One side of the room was filled with lighthouse equipment. Large concrete slabs held two enormous generators for running the foghorn. The radio beacon station took up several more feet of space, and a large, old-fashioned office desk occupied another wall. On the other side of the room was a panel of switches and buttons for operating the remote control of various lights, the foghorn and the fog bell.

"We'll have to build a partition across this room," Cy said. "We can put bunk beds and a highboy dresser on the smaller side, for Doug and Bruce."

"Won't the generators keep them awake?"

Cy had turned on one of them to let me hear the roar they made. He shook his head. "All we can do is try it," he said. "Maybe they'll get used to the noise. We'll see."

We bought large sheets of Hard-board and, after building a wooden frame from floor to ceiling, we nailed on the panels, covering the places where they came together with narrow wooden strips. Cy put a door between the Watchroom and their little bedroom. At least they would have privacy, even if it wasn't soundproof.

Then came the day to try out the pump. Cy carried the motor down to the pumphouse, and connected it to the pump. Holding our breath and saying a little prayer, we were ready to pull the switch. So much depended on running water. Would it work? Well, it began to hum! So far-so good.

"Run up and turn on a tap," Cy cried excitedly.

I wasted no time. Up I ran, and into the bathroom, where I turned on the tap of the wash basin. Water ran out — wonderful canal water; rusty-coloured, after all these years of non-usage, slightly fishy-smelling canal water; but water! I screamed for joy!

Cy ran up then, and, after switching on the heater for the hot water tank, he announced, "All's well; we'll have hot water in about half an hour. It'll clear up after it runs a while. That's from the rusty pipes. We won't want to use it for drinking, or cleaning our teeth, but it should be fine for bathing, laundry, and boiling vegetables."

"And flushing the toilet," I interjected, with a happy smile.

"It should be pretty good, really, We're just far enough out in the lake to get good water; you'll see." And he was right!

It took us a whole day to tear out the old hand pump and counter. We replaced these with a new kitchen sink and taps, and a new counter, covered with tile. Cy made connections with the water pipes, and, after digging a narrow trench across the road, put a drainage pipe from the kitchen to the canal.

What little time I had at home was spent sewing crispy, ruffled curtains. It was really unbelievable what we had accomplished in a week! With the windows sparkling, the venetian blinds in place, the curtains up, the whole house took on a most inviting appearance. There were still three days left before the canal opened for navigation, but we were ready to move to the lighthouse. Doug and Bruce were eager helpers. Into cartons we packed dishes, silver, cooking utensils and books. The movers took care of the rest. None of us felt too happy, but we tried to be cheerful, and made little jokes as we worked.

We moved on the Friday, and by eleven that night we had everything nicely arranged in the rooms, and we were eager to begin our new life.

Chapter Five
WE VISIT OLD WELLAND CANALS

We all awakened with the birds the next morning. The boys were eager to explore. Although Cy and I were very tired, we had the long weekend to relax, for the canal wouldn't open until Monday morning. Cy had a happy thought.

"How about a tour of the old canals?" he asked. "We could start at Port Dalhousie, the entrance to the very first Welland Canal."

"Oh, I think that would be wonderful," I said. "What d'you say boys? We'll start early, and make a day of it."

"Sure," they agreed. "Come on, let's go."

Everyone helped with breakfast, for we were all eager to be on our way. A friend had lent us a map of the old canals, showing the route to follow, and points of interest. We were soon in the car, and on our way to Port Dalhousie, just a few miles away.

We walked along the sandy beach at "Port," studying the map as we went.

"Here it is!" Cy called. "Look over here." We ran to join him, and exclaimed with delight on finding the exact spot of entry to the First Welland Canal. Following the route on the map, we found remains of the locks of the Second and Third Canals. Old wooden stumps, blackened and rotted over the years, stood out from the water, in rows, reminders of old piers, dock walls and other structures. This was near the mouth of the Twelve-Mile Creek. Directly across the creek was a large concrete grandstand, where crowds now sit to watch the Royal Canadian Henley Regatta.

"Was it like this when you used to row in the Regatta, Dad?" asked Doug.

"Yes, very much the same, except there was an old wooden grandstand in those days."

"How long has the Henley been held here, Dad?" Bruce asked.

"I believe it was brought here in 1903, when Port Dalhousie was named the permanent site for the races."

"Remember what Port Dalhousie was like when we were kids, dear?" I said, as we looked at the harbour of the Third Canal, the one that had been in operation throughout our younger days.

"I sure do," said Cy. "This was a marvellous place to come for family picnics. Why, steamers loaded with people used to come from Toronto and Hamilton, for annual outings!"

16

"How about the Emancipation Day crowds?" I reminded him. "Thousands of Negroes came here on that day to celebrate their emancipation from slavery. Some of them came hundreds of miles, and they had a glorious time."

Driving or walking, according to the terrain, we found stone ruins of old locks in the deep valley that still winds lazily through the western area of St. Catharines.

"Ah," I exclaimed. "Here's where your father and I used to come canoeing, when we were young." This was a section of the Twelve-Mile Creek that was particularly beautiful, with grassy banks and shade trees lining both sides of the creek.

"Yes," Cy added, "and there were always families sitting along the creek with fishing poles and picnic baskets."

Eearly Shipping in St. Catharines Welland Ship Canal Pt. Dalhousie Harbour 1895

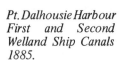

Pt. Dalhousie Harbour First and Second Welland Ship Canals 1885.

"It's still a very lovely spot." said Doug. Just then he exclaimed, "Look! There's our Sea Cadet land ship!"

Yes, there was the "Renown," where our boys went each week to learn seamanship, and practise rowing. Directly opposite this, on the other bank of the stream, Cy pointed out a tunnel built into the hillside.

"That tunnel leads underground to an opening beneath a large building, several hundred feet away. I've always understood that in the early days, slaves, escaping from the United States into Canada, would hide in small vessels until they reached this place, then scurry through the tunnel to a shelter that had been built for them in St. Catharines."

Doug and Bruce were wide-eyed at this information, but I had heard about it myself, in fact I remembered old Aunty Defoe, a wee, wrinkled old lady, whom everyone knew as a former slave. She was said to be over one hundred years old!

At this point in our travels, we came to part of the creek that ran very swiftly. Here, several factories still operated on the banks of the "Twelve."

Another turn in the stream revealed some old buildings — the remains of the once-famous Shickluna Shipyards.

"Shipbuilding was one of St. Catharines' chief industries in the old days," Cy told us. "Louis Shickluna came to Canada from Malta, in the early 1800 s. He was the answer to the settlers' dream; an experienced shipbuilder who could supply one of their most urgent needs. He was kept busy repairing and re-conditioning old canal boats for the Welland Canal, besides building new ships of many shapes and sizes. All traffic on the Welland Canal passed by his shipyard."

Back into the car, we drove beside the stream where it widened and turned towards Merritton and Thorold. This was where the First Canal climbed the Escarpment. At Merritton, we found remains of old wooden locks. They seemed too small to accommodate anything but pleasure boats of our day. Old stone cottages near the locks, reminded us of lock masters of olden times.

At Thorold, above the Escarpment, we found a number of old locks and weirs, and at Port Robinson we discovered more evidence of the old canals.

"Y'know," said Cy. "this place was once the hub of all canal activity."

We found this hard to believe, for now it was nothing more than a few old houses and run-down, empty shops.

"Yes," he continued, "Port Robinson was the chief port in the old days. It was the transfer point; the terminus of many coach lines, and the collection office for tolls. In those times, the price of land around Port Robinson was higher than land in Buffalo, New York!"

Back in the car, we followed the Welland River, winding lazily eastward to its terminus at Chippawa, on the Niagara River. Thus, we had travelled the entire route of the First Welland Canal. The turbulence of the Niagara River, however, had made it necessary to alter the original course of the canal.

"We'll drive back to Welland," said Cy, "and I'll try to find the place where they diverted the canal. They cut a channel due south, to Port Colborne, on Lake Erie, making this a more direct route from one lake to the other. This meant crossing the Welland River, just north of Welland, Ontario. A stone aqueduct was made, to carry the river under the canal. I understand that the aqueduct was replaced in later years by a concrete inverted syphon culvert, just north of the old aqueduct. Maybe we'll be able to find both of them."

"Gee, Dad," said Doug, "that must have been tricky; building a canal across a river."

"Yes, it was," Cy agreed, "but we'll see something even more amazing on our way back home. I've never see it myself, but I've been told it was a great feat of engineering, especially in those days."

The boys tried to pry the secret out of him, but Cy decided to keep it for a surprise. We drove along a road on the east bank of the canal. This section, the longest stretch of level water; sixteen miles, has been in use for three, later, canals; each one an improvement over the other.

As we drove along the pleasant wooded waterway, we noted remains of the former canals; especially that section of the Third Canal now used as a ship graveyard. Outdated ships are often scrapped here.

At last we came to Port Colborne, the Lake Erie terminus of the Welland Canals. It was a busy little town with little evidence of the old days. High-rising grain elevators lined the harbour, which is quite different from the one at Port Weller.

The lighthouse and smaller buildings were out on a concrete breakwall, running at right angle to the harbour. These must be reached by boat. As there was a considerable amount of floating ice on the lake, we knew there wasn't the slightest chance of getting out to see it.

"What a disappointment!" I exclaimed. "It would have been such fun to look around. I'd just love to meet the lightkeeper."

"Now Ethel," said Cy, shaking his head in mock exasperation, "y'know the station isn't open for navigation yet. Anyway, the keeper is an old fellow; almost ready for retirement."

"Oh," I said, "what marvellous stories he could tell!"

We then toured the area, noting Lock 8, the last lock in the Fourth Welland Canal. "This is the longest lock in the world!" Cy told us. We were all properly impressed.

We were also very hungry by this time, so we found a small restaurant, and had lunch.

Homeward bound, we followed the present canal to the Flight Locks at Thorold. Just before we came to the locks, we saw a guard gate and a safety weir, about three quarters of a mile from Lock 7. "This," Cy explained, "is an extra precaution for the double gates on Locks 6 and 7 — just in case a ship should get out of control at this point."

19

We passed Lock 7, which is at the summit of the climb up the mountain. Then came the wonderful Flight Locks, 4, 5 and 6.

"These twin locks, in one flight, have a total lift of 139½ feet. The east and west locks are separated by a concrete wall 60 feet wide. Here, ships can pass each other, being carried up or down the canal at the same time" Cy told us.

Below the Flight Locks, we crossed the canal over Bridge 5. Parking the car, Cy announced, "From here we must walk." By the expression on his face, we knew this was going to be our surprise. We trudged through brush and high weeds, walked perilously over a trestle bridge that spanned the Third Canal, and climbed up a steep bank, to find the old canal still filled with water. It looked like a fine place for a picnic or fishing in the summer.

Suddenly Cy yelled, "There it is! Look down!" He pointed to a spot below where we were standing. We tried to follow him as he scrambled down the bank, as fast as his legs could go. There, in a clearing, was a railway track. It seemed to run smack into the canal bank. We caught up to Cy, when he came to a stop and stood, shaking his head in wonder.

"Well," he said. "I'd never have believed it!"

By this time we, too, stood in amazement, looking into the mouth of a railway tunnel that apparently ran right under the Third Canal.

"Did trains really run through there?" asked Bruce.

"Yes, they did. It was the Great Western Railway. According to this map, it's been here for nearly one hundred years. Very few people know about it, as it's off any regular roads. I've lived here for nearly forty years and I had never heard about it."

A single track had been laid at right angles to the proposed site of the Third Canal. A cut-stone, arch-like tunnel, 635 feet long, 16 feet wide and 18 feet high was then built to house the railway lines. Earth and stone were piled over all but the opening at either end. The canal was then built above, and while ships sailed through the canal, trains ran through the tunnel below.

The stonework in the tunnel seemed to be in good condition, and, although there was some leakage from the water above, we could see through it for some distance, until it came to a bend.

"Oh, Boy!" yelled Bruce. "If only I had my rubber boots! I'd love to run right through it!"

"Maybe we'll come back some day," Cy suggested. We returned to the car, tired, but terribly excited about our discovery.

As we drove along the canal road, heading for home, Cy and I recalled what it was like on the Third Canal, when we were young.

"I learned to swim in the canal," said Cy. "We boys used to undress on the canal bank, and dive into the water in the nude. Oh, every once in a while some woman would let out a scream, at the sight of us but we just laughed. We weren't supposed to swim in the canal, but we did."

"I remember my father taking me for walks up Lake Street, to watch the ships sail through the canal," I told them. "We'd walk along well-worn towpaths, where horses and mules used to pull ships through the old canal. They sailed through under their own steam when I was a girl, and the old locks were operated by hand. Even the swing gates and bridges were opened and closed manually in those days. Later they were operated by electricity."

"Gee," said Doug, "It's hard to imagine what it was like in those days."

"Did you ever see a ship being pulled by horses, Dad?" asked Bruce.

"No, but many older people in this area can remember those days. Sometimes young boys would be allowed to ride on a canal horse, as it pulled a ship through the canal. 'To have the nerve of a canal horse,' was a favourite expression in the old days."

"In the summertime," I continued, "the canal banks would be crowded with picnickers and fishermen. Many people rode the towpaths on horseback, and there was always lots of activity along the canal.

"At that time the ships sailing the Great Lakes were becoming so large, many of them were unable to use the canal, for the locks were too small to hold them. Sometimes, the bow of a down-bound ship was pressed against the lower gates of the lock, and the stern shoved from one side to the other, to enable the upper gates to be closed, and the water drained, so the ship could drop to the next level."

"Sometimes a ship would knock out a lower gate," said Cy, "and flood the land below. The ship, then out of control, would end up stuck in the muddy bank of the canal. These wooden gates were all operated by hand, and it was a great responsibility. Sometimes the ships were so large, they had to be cut in two, in order to pass through the waterway!"

"I remember when word came to all the schools that a German submarine would pass through the canal," I said. "It was shortly after the end of World War I, and none of us had ever seen a submarine. All the children were marched to the canal to witness this exciting event. Great care was taken by the teachers to shepherd all the youngsters, but when it was time to return to school, one child was missing — It was my little brother, James! Well, the whole city was alarmed, and everyone, it seemed, joined in the search for the missing boy. Then he was found, sitting in a secluded spot on the canal bank, fishing!"

"It was always a worry for parents, to have this waterway so near their homes," said Cy. "Even in the winter, when it was frozen, there were drownings. Men would be cutting blocks of ice to store until the warm weather came, and danger signs would be posted, but sure as fate, some youngster would skate too close to thin ice, and fall through."

"Well, gang," announced Cy, "we're nearly home."

We had just turned to drive down the hill towards the lighthouse. "I'm ready for a good hot cup of tea!" I cried.

"It's been a lot of fun," said Doug. "I sure know a lot more about the canal and our history."

"Maybe our lighthouse will make history one day," Bruce said, thoughtfully.

"I don't know about you fellows," I said, "but I'm proud of our little bit of Canada."

"Yes," said Doug, "and somehow I feel better about moving to the lighthouse."

"Me, too," said Bruce. "Boy, what a lot of things I can tell the guys on Monday!"

Chapter Six

WE BEGIN LIFE AT THE PORT WELLER LIGHT

Doug and Bruce, who had been reluctant and hesitant about our move to the lighthouse, now had an entirely different outlook. They began to accept their new life with good humour. They were keen to try a hand at everything.

"I can hardly wait for the warm weather," said Bruce. "Bet I'm the first one to dive in the canal!"

"You'll have to get up early in the morning to beat me!" said Doug.

"I'll beat both of you!" Cy boasted.

"That lets me off the hook," I told them. "You won't get me into the water before the middle of July!"

"How about that great big sand pile up the road?" said Doug. "I can just imagine all the kids we know having a ball running up to the top and sliding down."

"I don't think we'll see many kids down here," I said, "that is, unless someone drives them down."

"They can ride down on their bicycles," Doug suggested.

"I doubt if they'll want to ride seven miles down here and back," I told them.

"We're going to do that . . . " said Bruce, "and five days a week, too." He paused a moment, then added, "what'll we do when it rains?"

"Don't worry about that, dear," I told him. "There's a bus to town, once you get to the main road. I'll drive you to catch the bus on bad days, and wait for you at the bus stop when it's time to come home." They were both visibly relieved to hear this.

Climbing the high tower was the boys' chief attraction. They teased me unmercifully, because I was afraid to try it. "Come on, Mother, it's a breeze. Just take one step at a time. You'll love the view from the top. You could even see Toronto!"

"Not I," I told them, "never, never, never!"

Finally, when Cy joined in the teasing, I was shamed into it. I reached the first landing safely, then stalled. Cy, with both arms outstretched for protection, was just one step behind me. I took a deep breath, said a quiet prayer, and climbed on. Each step was taken in terror. At last we reached the halfway platform. To go up or down, which was the more frightening?

"Come on, honey," urged Cy. "You're bent over like a pretzel; straighten up and don't look down."

23

I sucked in another deep breath, gritted my teeth and managed to climb to the top. There, I was above the treetops. What a wonderful sight from that lofty tower! I could see the western outline of the lake as it circled from Port Weller to Toronto, thirty miles away, and to the east was the shoreline all the way to Niagara.

The lake looked peaceful and endless as it blended into the horizon. Only one small ship could be seen — the sandsucker, "Charles Dick."

I gazed in wonder at the main light, while Cy told me all about it. The main light with large parabolic reflector was attached to a gear-driven table which revolved in a bowl of mercury. It revolved at a pre-determined rate to identify the light as Port Weller. Flashes from the light could be seen for twenty miles on a clear night. The light was very old and had originally been driven by a clock motor powered by weights. It had now been converted to electric drive, and was operated by remote control from the Watchroom.

Cy oiled the motor, checked the light bulbs, then said, "Ready, dear?"

"As ready as I'll ever be," I answered, and, following him, turned, facing the steps, and began the long, slow descent. The boys below cheered me on but the steps felt slippery, and my hands were clammy with sweat as I gripped the metal rails. Once again on the ground, I swore, "Never again!"

It was exciting watching for the first ship to enter the canal. I saw some in the distance, heading for other ports; then, suddenly, I saw one heading right for the opening to the canal, and then it slowly sailed right past the lighthouse. I stood on the bank, waving madly, and at last one of the sailors returned my wave. The captain of this ship would be honoured in an official ceremony in which he would receive a top hat for being the first to enter the canal that season. At first the movement of lake ships was slow, due to ice conditions in Lake Erie. It was at least two weeks later when the ocean ships arrived.

One day Cy called down to me from the top of the main light tower, "Look out in the lake, honey. It's the first Saltie!"

Sure enough, a short time later, a ship from The Netherlands sailed up the canal. The next one was a British ship; then one from Norway. It was easy to spot the salties from a distance, for they were quite different. They were smaller than most of the lakers, and rode higher in the water. My little camera was never far away, for I wanted to capture these exciting events on film.

Once the days grew warm, I was anxious to have a garden. The ground around the lighthouse was impossible to level by hand. We worked for days with pick and shovel to no avail. Finally, we had to give up.

"I'll have to get the canal bulldozer," said Cy. "We'll never be able to move this ourselves."

A few days later, a man arrived with his machine and levelled the ground all around. Now came the job of raking and digging. What an assortment of refuse we found! Railway spikes, nuts and bolts and sundry other items left by the canal builders! We decided to plant a vegetable garden first. How we watched for the first tender shoots of lettuce and beans to appear!

One morning, I ran outside, as usual, to note the growth, and screamed in anger, "There's nothing left!"

Cy came running, the boys close behind. "What's the trouble?" he asked. Then one glance told him. "It's those darned rabbits," he cried, "they've eaten everything!"

No matter what we planted, the rabbits ate it as soon as it showed above the ground; they even ate the bark off our rose bushes. It was hopeless to try any more. We settled for lawns and spirea bushes.

Cy was responsible for the operation of the station twenty-four hours a day. I helped him by taking the day watch, so that he could get some sleep. Except for stormy days, the boys rode to school on their bicycles. I drove into town once a week for groceries; then stopped for a short visit with our parents, for we had always lived close by our families, and I knew they missed us; especially the boys. We were told it was impossible for us to get a telephone, out on the pier, so I couldn't even call them. Sometimes the hours seemed to drag.

One day I asked Cy, "Could we have some chickens, dear?"

"What? — and have them blown into the canal the first windy day!"

It was quite true. On calm days it is so easy to forget the wild ones. When that west wind blows across the lake, it has a clean sweep of about 15 to 30 miles. Often, the bed sheets have been torn right out of my hands as I tried to take them off the clothesline.

Our house was about twenty feet from the canal, and the lake about a hundred yards to the west. No matter where we looked, we saw water. Sometimes, especially in rough weather, it was just like being aboard a ship. At least we were spared the rocking motion, but we often got the spray.

Every morning, once the porridge was made and the coffee "perking," I'd awaken the boys, then run through the woods to the lakeside. I just loved being out in the early morning air. Each day the view seemed different — the cloud formations, the various shades of colour in the sky and water. Taking deep breaths, and letting the wind blow my hair, I'd scan the horizon.

"Mother's out looking for bodies!" the boys would tease. I'd have died if I had ever seen anything as gruesome as that, but I must admit I was always on the lookout for something exciting.

The view from our pier was an ever-changing delight. From my favourite vantage point, about halfway down the pier, and looking westward, I could see, first, Port Weller Beach; then Port Dalhousie piers; and from there, the lake outlined in a giant semi-circle by the Niagara Escarpment, which shelters the whole Niagara Peninsula. During a temperature inversion, the entire shoreline, from Port Weller to Toronto, thirty miles away by lake, is clearly visible, and, at night, one can see lights all around the lake like a diamond horseshoe. The hills outlined by the sunsets, are magnificent, and the reflections from the steel furnace fires in Hamilton are the most spectacular sight of all.

One day, as I was standing there, a ship suddenly exploded! I ran, screaming, into the house. "I just saw a ship blown to pieces!" I yelled to Cy. He ran outside, and, with his binoculars, could see pieces of wreckage floating about. He radioed the shore station on Toronto Island, to notify all ships.

Within an hour we were besieged by hundreds of people, including the Press. Reports of the incident had been received from nearby beaches. All ships were accounted for except an oil tanker. Everyone assumed it was the casualty. Rescue planes and coastguard boats searched the area. In the debris was found a man's wallet, containing his name and address. This was the only clue to the disaster. When police called his home, they heard facts of a puzzling story. Two men, partners in a shipping business, owned an obsolete ship. They decided to take it out on the lake, set explosives, and blow it up.

After leaving the ship they pulled away in a small rowboat, and rowed to Port Weller Beach; watched the explosion, then took a taxi to their homes, unaware of the confusion they had caused, or simply unconcerned. If it hadn't been for the tell-tale wallet which had accidently fallen from one man's pocket, we may never have known the true story.

My woman's curiosity, or nose for adventure, kept me alert for any signs of unusal events: a small boat in distress; youngsters adrift on a home-made raft, or swimmers who had gone beyond their depth. These things happened all the time. Cy was always nearby, ready and willing to offer assistance, or radio for help, if it was beyond our means.

Storms seemed more frightening out there than at home in the city. They developed so swiftly, seemingly out of nowhere, and there was little time for the unwary to reach the safety of shore, but the fog was our worst enemy. It was deadlier than any storm, for it crept in without warning. A sudden change in wind or temperature caused the fog to roll its blanket in seconds. No warning instruments told us it was coming; only constant vigilance, that must be maintained twenty-four hours each day.

Sometimes fog is but a momentary thing; again, it can linger for a week or so without letup. The noise of the generators, pumping air into the foghorn, was deafening, for they sat plunk in the middle of our house. The radio beacon sending code, and the foghorn's mournful bellowing, sending its warning to ships on the lake, sometimes nearly sent Cy and me out of our minds. Strangely though, the boys, who slept so close to all the machinery, vowed they never missed a good night's sleep!

Inside or outside the house, there was no escape from the noise. During a very dense fog, if there were a few moments of silence, it was almost frightening, for the silence was pregnant with hidden fears. In such a fog, even the birds were still. It took me a long time to accustom myself to these strange and awesome periods.

In time I accepted these unpleasant days and learned to carry on with my household tasks, and simply ignore the noises and the depressing feeling of claustrophobia. I never realized the extent of dampness that pervaded the house until I noticed the veneer finish peeling off the bedroom furniture!

I was by nature a very timid person, having been afraid of electric storms;

going alone into dark places, and with a genuine dread of physical injury. Amazingly, this new life at the lighthouse helped me to control these fears; not all at once, but gradually, over the years. Tippy, who had been such a wonderful companion and protector during the war years had to be restrained in all his natural impulses. At first he would bark like crazy at small wild creatures or any unusal noise, but owing to Cy's peculiar sleeping hours, we had to re-train him to keep quiet; especially when in the house. On several occasions we had reason to regret this training.

Chapter Seven
THE PERILOUS WOODS

Many thousands of trees had been planted after the canal was built to beautify the banks and to provide shelter for ships plying back and forth along the waterway. There were trees from other countries, brought here as an experiment, to see how they would fare in this environment: olive trees, willows, shimmering aspen and every variety of evergreen; and here and there an apple or peach tree, planted unwittingly, no doubt, by youngsters on a camping trip or young lovers having a picnic lunch.

I loved the woods that surrounded our lighthouse but somehow never overcame my feeling of apprehension at being hemmed in by such a dense growth.

The boys made light of my fears. Maybe they were a little nervous themselves at times but they would never allow me to know that.

One morning, after the boys had left for school, I was keeping watch for Cy, who had been on duty fourteen hours that night. It was a soggy day, grey with fog. The foghorn was wailing and the radio beacon was beeping out its warning code signals.

Suddenly I heard an unusual, ominous sound. I took a frightened glance through the window. The fog had thickened and it was impossible to see more than a few feet through waves of mist.

As I continued to strain my eyes in one direction and then another, I was startled nearly out of my wits!

A row of men — about fifty of them, each one holding a shotgun, advanced towards the lighthouse, in the clearing. As they marched closer, like soldiers in battle, I held my hands over my mouth to keep from screaming!

One man, apparently seeing my frightened face at the window, hurried over, and beckoned me to the door. "I'm sorry we've upset you, Ma'am," he said. "We're hunting for rabbits. Y'know these piers were fenced off during the war. We weren't allowed to hunt through the woods. The rabbits have almost overrun the place, and we're flushing them to the end of the pier."

I dropped into a chair, wet with perspiration, and heaving a deep sigh of relief.

Later, when I told Cy about the incident, he was very upset. "Why didn't you call me?" he asked. His face flushed angrily. "Remember, Ethel, we're all alone out here. Who knows what danger is hiding in the woods?"

After that came weeks of foggy weather. The horn blew constantly, and our nerves were frazzled.

About eight-thirty one morning, I had just finished washing the breakfast dishes, and went outside, hoping to see the outline of a ship through the fog. There came a crackling sound from the direction of the woods. I held my breath. It wasn't — it couldn't be? — It was!

Advancing towards me came a line of men, just as before; shoulder to shoulder and carrying guns!

Trembling with fear, I froze to the spot. Then I noticed that some of the men wore police uniforms. One approached me.

"Have you seen a prowler, Mrs. Williamson?" he asked. — a young man in a swim suit?

"N--no, — I haven't." My voice quaked with fear. "What's going on? What has he done?"

"It's the Hatchet Murderer from Toronto," he explained. "He was seen swimming from a motor boat near the pier. A fisherman saw him climb the bank and disappear in the woods. He recognized the fellow from a photo in the newspaper."

With that, the man waved towards the others and they marched on towards the pierhead, like the hunters chasing rabbits.

Cy came running out of the house in alarm. When I told him about the fugitive, he pulled me inside the kitchen. "Lock all the windows and doors!" he shouted. "I'm going to make sure he's not lurking around here!" He loaded his gun and went outside.

I did as I'd been told then waited fearfully for Cy to finish his search.

Soon, he returned, shaking his head. "He's not hiding here," he said. "I'll keep the gun handy, just in case."

An hour later the posse came back. "We didn't find him," the police chief told us. "Keep your eyes open for the next day or so. You never know; he might be hiding nearby."

I never learned of the murderer being caught. It was weeks before I found enough courage to venture outside the house alone.

Chapter Eight
LOCKED OUTSIDE IN A STORM

A rush of cold air swept through the kitchen as Cy came in the door. He was furious. It was twenty minutes before sunset, and he had turned on the lights; then gone out to check them. His cheeks were burning red and his eyes flashed with anger.

"Those crazy hunters have shot out the green light again!" he shouted. "I'll have to drive over to the east pier and fix it right away."

"Oh, no!" I cried, feeling sick at the thought of it. "It's going to storm. I hate being alone in a storm. Will it take long?"

Cy shrugged his shoulders. "I won't know till I get there." He put his toolbox into the car trunk, and also a large carton of special light bulbs. "Keep an eye on the weather," he warned. "It looks black over the lake." He drove off in a hurry, after an anxious backward glance and a wave of his hand. The light must be repaired before dark. Due to the impending storm it was darker than usual at this time.

Doug and Bruce were having supper with their grandparents that night, for it was Friday, and they would go to Sea Cadets. Our meal, a casserole, would keep warm in the oven. It was no use feeling perturbed. The safety of the ships must always be our chief concern.

The two piers, extending so far into the lake, like giant arms, would be a hazard to shipping on the lake, whether headed for Port Weller, or sailing past, unless well-marked by special, identifying lights. As soon as visibility was reduced to a certain degree, pierhead lights flashed on automatically. A red light marked the west pierhead, a green one the east.

Checking on the weather through the kitchen window, I screamed out, "Oh my sheets!" The strong wind was blowing them horizontally. They were straining at the pins. Suddenly, one broke loose, flying from a single pin.

Not stopping for a coat, I dashed outside. Jumping into the air, I clutched at the sheets, which were twisted around the line. Now I felt the first drops of rain. There, I had the last sheet. I ran to the house. I must turn on the foghorn. Suddenly I panicked. The door had blown shut. I knew, even before trying, that the inside lock was on. I was locked out! This was horrible! I had to get inside. I just had to!

Anchoring the sheets to the ground with a big rock, I ran around the house, looking for an open window. I should have known better, for hadn't I closed them when the first dark clouds appeared? Away in the distance I could barely see Cy's figure, straddling the east light tower. There wasn't the slighest chance of attracting his attention to my plight.

He must be wondering why I hadn't turned on the horn. I was his trusted helper. I had never failed him before; I mustn't now! Angry tears of desperation streamed down my face and I pounded my fists together as I sought to find a solution to my dilemma.

The storm gathered momentum. Ships, from freighters to tiny pleasure boats, would be speeding to safe harbours. Each one depended on aids to navigation such as ours.

My job, as Cy's helper, was to watch for thickening weather if he was busy making repairs on the equipment or having a sleep. All I had to do was push a button or pull a switch. A simple chore like that — and here I was locked out and helpless!

The wind howled from across the lake. The black clouds were closing in. The storm would break any minute now. I looked towards the pierheads. The red light was flashing but there was still no sign of the green one. Cy must be having his troubles too. He would surely know by this time that something was wrong at the lighthouse but he couldn't come back until the green light was repaired. It was just as important as the horn.

I knew how anxious he must be. There must be a way to get inside that house. But how? That was the question.

The building was made of poured concrete, a foot thick. The steel-framed windows were made to withstand storms and blizzards, and were bolted from the inside. The solid oak doors could resist a giant. Breaking into that lighthouse would be like attacking a fortress. It would be impossible.

Suddenly I thought of the bathroom window. Sometimes it was closed but the bolt left unfastened. I must make sure; it was my only chance. I ran to the west side of the house and looked up at the window. It was closed all right, but it was difficult to see if the bolt was fastened. I must climb up and try it.

I found some wooden boxes; dragged them beneath the window and climbed up. The window ledge was about five feet off the ground. The window, six feet high, was only twenty inches wide, and the only part that moved was a centre pane, halfway up the window and set in a separate steel frame. This centre pane could be pushed forward or backward at right angles by means of a metal pin across the middle. This allowed an opening at either the top or bottom half of about twenty inches by eight, less the metal frame. I was too low to try!

Now my problem was to climb high enough to force myself through this opening; that would be only if the window was unbolted. I must find something else to climb on. Frantically I ran from one side of the house to the other. Then I saw a couple of cement blocks. With the strength of four women I dragged these to the window and lifted one on top of the other. I put the wooden boxes on top of these and up I went. I pushed on the pane of glass. It moved! Thank God!

Now, could I squeeze through? Well, I had to. Visibility was now less than three miles. A thousand crazy thoughts raced through my mind. What if a ship ran aground, or into a pier? It would be my fault, whatever happened.

How could I be so stupid? Imagine being locked out of my own house! I had to get inside somehow. At the same time I knew I was bigger than that opening. It would have been a tight squeeze for a thin girl; impossible for a plumpy one like me.

I slanted the pane downward, into the bathroom. Bending at the waist, and with arms outstretched, I thrust arms and shoulders through the upper opening, as if about to take a dive. Now I began worming myself inch by inch through the steel frame. In spite of the cold rain, I was feverishly hot. The frame's knife-like edges scraped my flesh, but I didn't even feel it. "Oh, Boy!" I thought, "this is one time I wish I were flat-chested!"

Bit by bit I inched myself through that narrow opening. There! I was in as far as my waist. What if I couldn't make it the rest of the way? I'd be in a fine fix wedged halfway through a window. Now I began to worry about my landing. The bath tub was at least six feet below me. I knew that once my hips were through my legs would offer no resistance. I'd drop like a ton of bricks. I tried to gauge my hands to make a fast grab for the sides of the tub to break my fall. I mustn't land on my head after all this effort.

Inch-inch-inch — suddenly it was all over! My hands clutched the tub rim with ease and I landed safely. Climbing out, I ran to the Watchroom and pushed the button for the horn. The generator roared into action, and a few moments later came the welcome, sonorous bellow of the foghorn. "Thank God!" I whispered.

Later, when I told Cy of my adventure, I had to join him in roars of laughter at the ludicrous spectacle I described. "Really, dear," I said, "I honestly don't know how I got through that window." An impish grin lighted Cy's face. He made a great show of measuring the approximate size of the window and then my own well-rounded proportions.

"I don't know, either," he said. "Figuratively speaking, it was quite impossible!"

On the subject of figures, I'm reminded of an amusing incident that happened on a hot day that summer.

I love to sew, but living "Far From the Madding Crowd" brought many unusual problems, among which was dressmaking. No longer could I call on a sister or friend to help fit a dress properly. Cy might help on occasions but he had little patience with these things.

"Why not buy a dress form?" he asked one day when I was upset about a fitting.

"Jiminy!" I answered, with some steam. "I would rather spend the $20 on material. I could make four or five dresses for that!"

"Wouldn't it be smarter to make one that really fit perfectly?" he asked, rather pointedly.

I tossed my head, feeling a little hurt at his touch of sarcasm, "I'll think about it," I said.

Later that same day I came across a large roll of adhesive paper, about an inch and a half wide. It was the kind of paper one must wet, like a stamp, and was used for sealing cardboard boxes. I showed it to Cy and asked, "How about helping me to make a dress form?"

He looked surprised, then said, "I don't get you, honey. What d'you mean?"

I explained. — "Well, — I once heard a girl tell about this in the beauty shop. You get someone to wet the paper, then wind it round and round your body in several layers. When it dries, it is cut up the middle of the back, slipped off, and Presto! — you have a dress form, exactly like you!"

"Won't it stick to your skin?"

"Oh, no. I forgot to tell you, one must wear a knit shirt underneath."

Cy looked skeptical. I had to coax him. "Come on, dear, be a sport; let's try it."

"OK, then. I'll get a bowl of water and a sponge while you undress."

I hurriedly slipped out of my clothes and pulled on one of Cy's T-shirts, size 42, which came down to my knees. I giggled while he began winding the wet stripping around my body. I didn't realize that I had forgotten one of the most important instructions — I should have worn an uplift brassiere under the shirt. Also, it would have been correct to begin the winding from the waist up, then down over the hips. Ah, well, ignorance is bliss. Cy started under the arms, then over each shoulder, and across the chest.

As the binding crept lower and lower, I had difficulty in breathing and my bust was flattened like a boy. Layer after layer was wound around me until I looked and felt like a mummy. I was so dizzy from turning around, Cy had to walk around me in circles, making sure were enough layers of paper to form a rigid shape when it dried. When we ran out of stripping paper we decided it would have to do.

"Now, what are you going to do?" asked Cy.

"Why, I'll just sit outside in the sun, and wait 'till it dries."

Cy burst out laughing, "Oh, Boy!" he exclaimed. "You've got more nerve than I!"

"There isn't a soul to see me." I told him, and, donning a large straw hat and sunglasses, I found a sunny spot behind the house. I tried to sit on a chair. I couldn't bend! "Oh, dear," I moaned, "I'll have to stand up. It might take hours!" I was really in a fix.

Trying not to laugh at my predicament, Cy attempted to console me, but, seeing through his pretence, I exploded with indignation. Fighting back my tears, I screamed: "Don't stand there making fun of me! Help me to lie down on the suncot!"

He actually had to lift me and place me horizontally on the cot, and there I stayed for more than two hours, slowly turning over to expose all sides to the sun's rays, and recalling memories of a country fair, where an oxen was barbecued on a turning spit, over hot coals!

Cy came out from time to time, managing to restrain his laughter at this comical sight. Finally, he decided I had suffered enough. He helped me to my

33

feet, and into the house, where, with scissors and an old straight razor, he slit my suit of armour straight up the back from thigh to neck. After some maneuvering and not a little wriggling on my part, we finally slipped it off, T-shirt and all!

Without a single glance, I dashed into the bedroom and donned a robe, then returned to the kitchen, where Cy had stood the molded shape on the table. He had closed the back opening with scotch tape. I took one look at it then screamed out in disgust, "That's not my shape! I know I don't look like that!" I was ready to cry, but Cy was laughing so hard by this time, I found it infectious. I bent over double, with gales of laughter.

"It's an hour-glass shape, honey," said Cy, "but all the sand's gone to the bottom!" Later, he said, "What will you do with it?"

"I'll show you," I replied, and, lifting it with both hands, I ran through the woods and threw the monster into the lake!

Chapter Nine
POWER FAILURE!

Everything had been running smoothly at the lighthouse, when, one night in the midst of a bad storm, lightning struck the main transformer that produced power for the whole canal!

Lights, radio beacon, foghorn, and all electrical equipment on the canal ceased to operate!

We lit oil lamps in the house but our chief concern was for the ships on the lake. Many of these were at anchor just off the pierheads. What if one of them accidently ran into a pier? It could be an oil barge or even one filled with gasoline! The possibilities were too awful to contemplate.

There seemed nothing to do but wait for the canal electricians to find the trouble and make repairs. Then Cy remembered seeing a huge box marked "auxiliary foghorn." Although the canal had been in operation for more than fourteen years this box had never been opened.

The box was stored in the room atop the main light tower. How could we get such a large, awkward object down those flights of steps in the dark?

"I'll have to awaken the boys to help me," said Cy. Although they were sleepy-eyed, both boys were eager to help.

"What can we do, Dad?" asked Doug. "We can't carry it down."

"No," said Cy, "but Bruce and I will go up with block and tackle. We'll tie it securely, then lower it slowly to the ground. I'll drop one end of the rope first, and you can lower it gently, so it will drop clear of the tower. Do you think we can do it? It's going to be a big job in this storm."

The boys had dressed by this time; they all wore rain coats and carried flashlights.

Cy insisted that I stay in the house, and fearfully, I watched from the bedroom window. In an amazingly short time the box was safely lowered to the ground, opened, and the foghorn lifted into the trunk of the car. "I can slide it out on boards," said Cy. "You fellows go back to bed; I'll manage."

Covered by his Airforce cape, carrying a thermos of tea, and with Tippy for company, Cy drove to the pierhead. There, after unloading the machine, he sat astride it, pumping the handle back and forth, producing mournful bellows in answer to the fog signals from the ships nearby, and showered by spray from the 15-ft waves that lashed across the pierhead.

Visibility was zero, and, although I worried about possible danger to the ships, my chief concern was for Cy, all alone in the storm.

35

About 3 a.m. power was restored. Everything came to life in an instant — lights, beacon, and the generator engine to blow the horn. I knelt on the kitchen floor and whispered, "Thank God!" Soon after, Cy arrived, soaking wet in spite of all his covers, and completely exhausted from his ordeal.

"Never again!" he exclaimed, as he peeled off his wet garments. "There must be a better way than that!"

Chapter Ten

MID-SUMMER FUN

Our first year of duty at the lighthouse brought many changes and improvements along the canal.

During the war, barbed wire fences and barricades built to protect the waterway had kept the public at a distance. These were now removed and people once more began taking an interest in canal watching.

Many of the first salties still bore the scars of sea warfare and were painted in sombre colours; some still wore camouflage. It wouldn't be long before new ships, specially built for sailing the Great Lakes, would make their appearance in colours to rival the rainbow.

From the earliest days St. Catharines had been known as a famous ship-building area. Vessels from Louis Shickluna's Shipyard on the "Twelve," sailed the Seven Seas, but that was over a hundred years ago. Now, a new shipyard was being built just above Lock 1, on the Welland Canal. The Port Weller Shipyards and Drydocks would become an enormous, thriving industry, bringing fame to St. Catharines and prestige to the whole Niagara District.

When the Fourth Welland Canal was built, it included a drydock for the maintenance of the canal's floating equipment. As the years passed by, the canal found little work for the drydock, and when a group of businessmen became interested in taking over control of it and expanding it into a ship building enterprise and drydock, the Department of Transport was agreeable to the venture.

Much of the work in the shipyards consisted of routine repairs of all kinds of vessels; the re-modelling and construction of ships and the conversion of antique barges into modern motor ships.

The shipyards were a beehive of activity, even in the winter. Many freighters went into drydock for repairs; others tied up nearby during the off-season months. Some of these were fully loaded, ready to begin sailing the moment the canal opened in the spring. A watchman, usually a member of the ship's company, would stay with the ship, often with his wife and small children aboard, for the living quarters were very comfortable.

Although there were no holidays at the lighthouse during the shipping season, Dominion Day, July 1st, turned out to be a very special day for us that first year. It brought our Lightship, the "Grenville." There was no mistaking her, for she looked like a pint-sized saltie, painted black with lots of white trim.

We all ran outside to greet her; waving our arms to the crew, as she anchored about a hundred yards from the shore. Doug and Bruce, now on their summer holidays, cheered aloud as a motor boat was lowered and began chugging towards the steps leading up the canal bank. They were already waterlogged from hours of swimming, and the "Grenville" brought the promise of something different and exciting. It was almost as thrilling as receiving a Christmas present. I must admit my own heart was pounding as the little boat touched the bank and two trimly-dressed officers climbed up the bank to meet us. One, Captain Morphet, skipper of the "Grenville" introduced Mr. Arthurs, an official from Prescott.

We had heard that Mr. Arthurs was a hard man to deal with, but both Cy and I found him most charming. Later, Captain Morphet invited us to tour his ship, which we were delighted to do.

Meanwhile, the crew was bringing boatloads of supplies from the ship. We had no idea of what was coming, for the order had been sent in by the former keeper, the year before.

It was a surprising collection: a ton of coal, gallons of lighthouse paint — red, white, green and battleship grey — cans of oil, corn brooms, mops, rags, pails, lightbulbs, soap, and first-aid supplies of iodine, band-aids, burn ointment and a great assortment of pills.

Then — a wonderful surprise — a rowboat!

"Hurray!" the boys screamed. "Now for some real fun!"

Everything from the Grenville had been left piled up on the canal bank. We all helped in sorting and carrying boxes, barrels and cans of paint to a small storage shed behind the house.

The boys urged us to try out the boat. We all lifted it into the water, then had a ball rowing back and forth.

"We can't leave it in the water," Cy said. "We'll have to build a dock of some kind."

"Let's go!" cried Doug. "There's lots of lumber around."

Luckily, a concrete piling had been planted in the canal, about fifteen feet from the water pump, It had been placed there to hold the metal pipeline that carried canal water into the pumphouse. The fellows built a trestle between the piling and the rocks, then, after building a plank walk, they carried it down to the trestle and secured it, by bolting it in place. Some sturdy hooks were fastened on the dock to be used for securing the boat, and we found a couple of old tires for bumpers.

Later that week the boys decided to row as far as a buoy near the canal entrance. The water was deeper there, for swimming.

As usual, Tippy jumped into the canal and swam after them. The faster they rowed, the swifter he swam. Realizing a lost cause, they finally stopped. Cy and I roared with laughter, as we saw Bruce haul him into the boat. "Now they'll get a shower," said Cy. Sure enough, when Tip shook himself, they were covered by spray. "They'll never outwit that dog," Cy chuckled.

The boys were strong swimmers, and they were accomplished rowers, having had lots of practice in Sea Cadets. We had no fears of them in the water. Little did we know the danger they would face that day.

Near 5 o'clock, supper was ready, and I went outside to look for the boys. As a rule their stomachs warned them when it was time to eat; especially these days with all their outdoor activities. There wasn't a sign of them in the canal. I returned to the kitchen.

About ten minutes later, worried, I called to Cy. "Have a look for the boys, dear. I've never known them to be this late for a meal."

Cy got his binoculars. "I'll go up the tower and have a look," he said.

"I hope they're all right," I called, as he began climbing up the steps.

"Here they come!" he called down to me. "They're running down the road! Something's wrong!" He hustled down the steps, and we both ran up the road to meet them.

Tippy was well ahead of the boys, but we soon reached them.

"What's the matter?" called Cy.

Both boys began talking at the same time. All we could make out of the chatter was, "That darn dog! — Crazy duck! — Didn't want to lose the boat!"

"Hold on, fellows," said Cy. "Now, try to make some sense out of this. First of all, are you all right? That's the main thing."

"We're fine, Dad," said Doug. "Scratched up a bit, but we're ok."

"The boat's safe, too," added Bruce. "But you'll never believe what happened."

"Ok, then, boys, let's have it. What did happen?"

Doug shook his head, then a broad smile lighted his face. He said, "Well, Dad, y'know Tip followed us, and we had to lift him into the boat. After our usual shower bath, he settled down, and we rowed to the buoy and tied up the boat. We dived into the canal and had a ball swimming all around, waving to the ships' crews and everything. We had lots of fun teasing Tippy, and we fooled around 'til we were really tired. We knew it was near supper time, so we climbed into the boat. Bruce was just lifting Tippy into the boat when we spied twelve little ducklings swimming by. They were so cute, I reached out and picked one out of the water, for a closer look."

Bruce interrupted at this point. "It was the cutest little thing I've ever seen, Mom. We've often seen them at a distance, but never close up like this."

Doug continued with his story. "The mother duck wasn't with them. We thought it strange. Suddenly, without warning, she dived down on us! She flapped her wings and scratched us with her claws. It was terrifying! She would fly up into the air for a few moments then nosedive right at the boat!"

"The worst part," said Bruce, "Was that we couldn't get away! We tried and tried to untie the boat from the buoy, but it was a tight knot, and she didn't leave us alone long enough to get it undone."

"That darn dog!" Doug exclaimed. "He was no help. Every time the duck came at us, Tippy barked like crazy, hopping over us, back and forth, as we crouched down in the bottom of the boat, trying to cover our faces and heads with our arms. It was awful!"

"I finally grabbed hold of Tip and threw him into the canal," said Bruce. "Then, the next time the duck flew away Doug managed to untie the boat."

"You should have seen us, Mom," said Doug. "We tried to row up the canal towards the lighthouse, but the duck kept after us. By this time we were close to the canal bank, so we decided to head for the rocks. While I rowed the boat, Bruce tried to fight off the bird with his hands. We were both afraid she'd peck our eyes out! She fought us all the way to the rocks. Tip was already out of the water, running back and forth on the canal bank, and barking like a wild dog. When we finally hit the rocks, I jumped out, grabbed the rope, and started to secure the boat. By this time Bruce was out too. The duck came at us again, but this time Tippy made a jump at her, and she flew away! We made sure the boat was safely tied to a big rock then climbed up the bank and headed for home."

"The boat's safe, Dad," said Bruce. "That's the main thing, and I still have the baby duck. Look!"

"To heck with the boat, Son," Cy said, huskily. "My boys are OK, that's what really matters, but don't you think you should give the duckling back to its mother?"

The next day, except for some scratches and bruises, the boys were fine. "One thing is sure," said Bruce, between mouthfuls of oatmeal porridge, "I'll never tell my pals I was beaten by a duck!"

What fun we had with that rowboat! Up and down the canal we would row, from the pierheads to Lock 1. The boys even went as far as Port Dalhousie, on a calm day. Together, we made sails of white canvas; a mast and a rudder. When it was finished, we all set out for a sail. A stiff breeze soon carried us mid-stream, then the boat began going in circles.

"I knew something was missing," said Cy, in disgust. "I forgot we had to have a keel!"

We had many summer visitors; most of them had never seen a lighthouse before. The first thing that intrigued them was the high light tower. They all seemed disappointed to find that we didn't live in the light tower, for it seems that everyone envisioned a lighthouse as I had at first: an enclosed, circular tower, with different levels, where the keeper and his family made their home. Just the same, our tall steel structure was most impressive, and the men and boys could hardly wait to climb up the steps to the top. One man barely reached the upper platform, when he collapsed. We never knew whether it was his heart or just shortness of breath, but he remained up there, lying on the platform, for more than an hour before daring to climb down.

Most of the girls who came to the lighthouse hadn't enough courage to climb the tower, but there was always the brave one who made the rest of us look like sissies.

Cy's brother, his wife, Margot, and their son, Robert came from California, to spend a month with us. Cy hadn't seen his brother, Ivan for six years. It was a joyful reunion, and we all had a happy time together.

They had travelled in a house trailer, so accommodations were no problem; they just parked the trailer in the woods, close to the house, and everything worked out fine.

The boys bought a used outboard motor, which they fastened to the boat, and they had a grand time in the canal. That rowboat brought us more hours of pleasure than anything we had ever owned. It was also handy if there was an emergency of any kind in the water, and it proved to be a much more expedient method of crossing the canal when the East Pierhead lights needed attention.

There seemed to be always something moving on the canal. Every ship that passed by was of interest to me. I soon got to know their names, and watch for their return. The passenger ships were beautiful. There were three of these making regular runs between the lakes — the North American, the South American and the Noronic. Hundreds of passengers in bright summer clothes lined the rails, as the ships sailed past our lighthouse. I always stopped my work to wave hello, and many of them returned my greeting. If they passed by after dark, the air was filled with gay dance music, and the hundreds of lights, reflecting on the water, made it look like fairyland.

One day Doug ran into the house, excitedly. "Mom," he cried, "there are two ponies on our dock. They're trying to get a drink of water!"

"How did they ever get here?" Bruce asked, as he dashed outside to see them. "I think they're from a circus," he said, as we stood on the bank above,

Bruce, Douglas and Tippy.

Skinny-Dipping in Canal.

41

not knowing just how to approach them. There was a frayed end of rope hanging from each pony's neck.

"Let's take them a couple of pails of water," said Cy. "By the look of them, they've been tied up without food or water. I'd better go down to them, in case they act wild." They lapped up the water in a hurry, and soon, holding onto their ropes, Cy was able to lead them up the steps. We petted them and fed them shredded wheat biscuits.

"I bet they're carnival ponies," said Doug. "Can we ride them, Dad?"

"You can try, but take it easy, they're probably frightened and skittish." The boys needed no further advice. They had once spent a holiday on a farm where there were several old race horses, and they had often ridden them bareback. Now they were off, trotting down the road and screaming, "Yippee!" like cowboys.

"I'm going to drive to town to pick up James's kids. They're just the right age for a pony ride. Won't they love it?" I said.

"By the way our boys acted, I'd say any age is just right for a pony ride," said Cy, smiling broadly. "You'd better hurry though. The owners must have missed them by now. I'd like to horse-whip them when they do show up. Imagine leaving poor dumb animals tied up without food or water. I'll see that the boys give them a good rest before you get back with the little ones."

About an hour later I returned with a car-load of excited youngsters, and my mother, who insisted she must have a ride, too. She was no bigger than the grandchildren, and just as thrilled as they.

There were screams of joy as we lifted each one on a pony's back. We walked along beside the smallest children, but the older ones trotted along without help. Cy had already been in touch with the Humane Society, through the canal phone, and later that day they came with a van and took them away.

Later that summer, a few sightseers, or, as we called them, canal watchers, came down our road, looking at the ships.

The public hadn't been allowed near the canal for more than five years, and many local people had really missed watching the progress of ships along the canal. They all hoped to see something unusual and exciting and quite often they invented excuses to get inside the lighthouse.

One day, in the pouring rain, there came a loud banging on the door.

I opened it and found a man who gestulated wildly with his hands as he talked. "Out in the lake!" he said, breathlessly. "Two men — clinging to a raft! They must have been shipwrecked!"

Cy grabbed his raincoat and binoculars, and followed the man through the woods to the lakeside.

"There, — there they are!" the man shouted.

Cy scanned the horizon for a moment or two, then, handing the glasses to his companion, he burst into loud guffaws of laughter. "Here, take a look at your shipwreck survivors!" he said.

After a brief glance through the glasses, the man returned them to Cy with an embarrassed grin. All he saw were two large seagulls, resting on a floating log!

*Douglas and Bruce in
Sea Cadets.*

Chapter Eleven

HAM RADIO – THE KEY THAT OPENS ALL DOORS

September, 1946. Doug and Bruce were back to school; summer visitors had gone, and the days grew long and lonely.

"Oh," I sighed, "if only I had a telephone!"

After running a beauty shop for years, with the constant buzz of voices: the humming of the hair dryers, and the ringing of the telephone, this solitude, this silence was awful. I had often yearned for peace and quiet, but this was too much.

While Cy was sleeping, I tried to keep busy by sewing, reading and braiding rugs, but what I craved was companionship, communication. Suddenly, I remembered Cy's old hobby, ham radio! Maybe that was the answer.

Cy had been a licenced amateur radio enthusiast from his early teens and, after our marriage, he built a radio room (hamshack) in his basement workshop. This proved to be a popular meeting place for many young men, who came to exchange ideas and to experiment with this fascinating pastime.

As a young bride, I resented this hobby which took up so much of his time. The squeaks and squawks, that came from downstairs meant nothing but noise to me. Often, in the long, lonely days after Cy left for overseas I regretted my former indifference to his hobby, and wrote, "If you come back safely, dear, I promise to learn all about ham radio, then we can share your hobby."

A letter from Cy, written about the same time, showed mental telepathy, for he wrote, "Darling, if I ever get back home to you, I'll never touch ham radio again! When I think of all the hours I wasted in the basement, when I could have been loving you, I could kick myself!"

Cy had kept his promise, but, as I sat in the lighthouse, frustrated and phoneless, with this terrible urge to communicate, amateur radio seemed the perfect answer to my need. Why not encourage Cy to rebuild his radio station, which had been dismantled at the outbreak of war? This way, we would have a means of chatting with our friends in town and allow us to talk to people in far-away places. Cy's prophecy could come true. Ham radio would be a blessing to us.

Cy was delighted with my interest in his hobby. Together we collected tubes, condensors and other components to be used in building an amateur radio station. I was an eager helper, happy to hold small parts and wires while Cy soldered them together. It all seemed like a giant jigsaw puzzle to me. Was it possible that all these bits and pieces would turn into a transmitter and receiver?

Now, what about an aerial? We ran a long wire antenna from the top of an obsolete electric pole to a point the same height from the ground, on the main light tower. Cy did all the climbing, and I kept the wire from tangling.

We then built a three-element rotary beam, and fastened it on top of a wooden tower, which Cy erected on the top of the house, and we were ready to go on the airwaves.

After hours of testing with local hams, we began seeking distant points. What a thrill it was to hear a voice from South America, England, France, Denmark, The Netherlands, and other lands!

Ethel operating our radio station in 1949.

From our very first contact over the air our lighthouse hamshack became a meeting place for men of every race, colour and creed! Cy tried to persuade me to say hello to some of his radio friends, but I always refused. I was terrified of the microphone. It was enough for me to be able to listen in on all these wonderful contacts, and I could hear both sides of the conversations in any room of the house. I was quite content — that was until the morning I heard Cy talking to a GIRL!

We knew that girls had been regular radio operators almost from the beginning, but they had used CW, or code. This was the very first one we had heard on phone. Excitedly, I ran from the kitchen, where I was preparing lunch, to the little corner of the Watchroom, where Cy was operating. He beckoned for me to take the microphone and talk to her. After a few terrifying moments, I relaxed, and soon found myself enjoying my first conversation on short wave radio. It was thrilling! After that, Nancy Archer of British Honduras and I had daily chats over the air.

I was really bitten by the "radio bug," zipping through my housework to spend hours on the radio.

The Department of Transport gave me special permission to talk on the air, without a licence, for we were classed as an isolated station, however, Cy must be on hand to operate the equipment. He had never been much of a "talker" preferring to work on experiments with the mechanical aspects of radio. It pleased him to find that I had at last come to love his hobby.

The moment I called "CQ" (an invitation to chat over the air) I would hear dozens of answers. I would then choose the one that sounded the most interesting. It might be Luxemburg, Belgium, Denmark, South America, Africa, the British Isles, or any place one could think of. As English is the universal language of ham radio, I was most fortunate. I, who had never travelled, was suddenly in personal contact with people all over the world! They asked questions about Canada, our lighthouse and our family, and I learned many interesting facts about them.

From that time on the days never seemed to have enough hours for me.

Many of our Canadian servicemen were still stationed in foreign countries. If they were near a ham radio station it was a wonderful chance to make contact with home. The moment they heard my friendly female voice from "home," they began calling our station. Would I give a message to their families? Could I contact a loved one by phone? How were things in Canada? If their family lived within a few miles — could I invite them to the lighthouse for a personal chat?

Well, not having a telephone, it was impossible to do some of the things I would have liked to do for the boys, but it was possible to contact another ham in the serviceman's hometown, and to make a schedule for him to be listening on the air at a specified time; then I hoped for the best. Sometimes I wrote to the relatives, making a date for them to come to the lighthouse at a certain time. When this arrangement turned out satisfactory, and the wife or parents could come for the schedule, it was the most rewarding time of my life.

Sometimes it was more than I could bear; hearing these conversations between loved ones, who were so many miles apart. I often felt like running from the room to hide my tears. I knew only too well the awful heartache of being separated from those we love.

Once, a retired army colonel and his wife came to talk with their soldier son in England.

The scheduled date and time had been arranged in advance. Now, everything depended on a clear air channel and good reception of signals.

The colonel and his wife arrived at the lighthouse nearly an hour early. Can you imagine how anxious and excited they felt at the prospect of hearing their son's voice, after an absence of four years? They had never heard of ham radio, and yet the fact that we had a station here and their son had an amateur friend over there, was going to make this contact possible. Several times I closed my eyes tightly and gave a silent prayer that everything would turn out all right.

Right on the dot, I called the station in England. Almost immediately, I received an answer. After a few preliminary remarks, the son greeted his parents. At first they were so overcome and nervous, I had to help them, but soon all fear vanished, and, with tears flowing from everyone's eyes, they were chatting away as clearly as if on a private telephone.

46

The daughter-in-law spoke briefly, then, the most touching moment of all . . . the unmistakable sounds of an infant child . . . their grandson!

That day I decided to become a licensed operator. I could have carried on for years in my present status, but that didn't satisfy me. I was determined to learn everything possible about my hobby, and have my own call sign.

Cy was delighted when I told him of my decision.

"It will mean a lot of studying," he warned. "It won't be easy. You'll have to learn International Morse Code, and reach the required speed of sending and receiving."

"What else will I need to know?"

"Well, I think your best bet is to buy the booklet, "How to Become an Amateur Radio Operator." It's only fifty cents, and I know it contains all the information you will need. You'll have to learn to draw diagrams of simple transmitters and receivers — I can help you with that."

"What about learning the code?"

"Oh, that won't be too difficult. All it takes is practice," he said. "I'll make you a practice set and key. We can take turns sending and receiving."

From the time I had my booklet, I began thinking of words as symbols of code. While setting the table for a meal, I'd sound out code letters for the salt, pepper, sugar and tea. Names of people also became code. For example, my own name was — dit---da---dit dit dit dit---dit---dit da dit dit.

Once I learned the alphabet in code, I then learned special groups, or radio combinations of letters. These symbols, --CQ---QRT---QSO---K--- and so on have the same meaning in every language, thus making it possible to communicate, at least in a limited way, with foreign hams who know little English.

I drove to Hamilton, passed my Government tests and was given a licence to operate a radio station, and the call sign, VE3DTW. This made me very happy, for Cy's call was VE3TW.

Every country has its own distinctive call signs. Canada is VE, and each province has a number; Ontario being No. 3. The final letters indicate one's own personal station. Having my own licence, meant that from now on I could operate alone during the hours when Cy was asleep. This was the beginning of a new life for me; an open invitation to make friends in every country in the world, and yet never leave the little radio corner of our lighthouse.

I was amazed at the number of people who spoke perfect English. There were, of course, many whose knowledge of English was very limited, but so anxious were they to communicate with hams in other countries, that they persevered, and I was more than delighted to help them out. After each contact, cards were exchanged, verifying the conversation, on a certain hour, day and year. Some of these cards I received were really comical. One from Natal, Brazil, started, "Dear Offal," and ended, "Here I am, at your disposal," and then came the signature, "Count Cavalcanti!" In all, Cy and I have contacted over 250 countries!

The American Radio Relay League, an international organization to which we belong, issues a certificate to hams working one hundred countries, confirmed. Other awards are available, and many hams strive to earn them, but my ambition was to make friends and share experiences. I loved to hear about life in far-away places. Every day brought new delights.

My knowledge of radio was also an asset to the lighthouse. Our radio beacon station was one of the most important aids to navigation. At regular intervals, it sent a code message to all the ships on Lake Ontario. This message, a "V" signal, was synchronized to play, within seconds, in alternate periods with two other stations, located at other points on the lake.

Ships on the lake use these radio signals to find their exact position. Any change in schedule; any trouble with the beacon could cause a jamming of signals from the other stations, bringing confusion to the whole system. These problems must be noted immediately, and corrected as soon as possible. While I was not qualified to touch the equipment, at least I was now able to detect the slightest change and report this to Cy.

It brought me pleasure to learn how people longed to hear all about Canada. I tried to give them a true picture, and was happy to answer their questions. "Why is your lighthouse so far from the sea?" "How is it possible for ocean ships to sail there?"

Often I'd be talking to someone in France, Holland or Denmark, and at that very moment I could see a ship from that country sail right by my front door! "One of these days," I would tell them, "many more ships from overseas will sail on the Great Lakes. The St. Lawrence Seaway will open the gates to larger ships than we've ever seen, but it won't come for many years."

With mixed emotions I watched the first German freighter sail by. Shortly after, I heard a knock on my door. It was a young man.

"Pardon me, Ma'am," he said, hesitantly. "I'm Bill Korff, the radio operator on the ship that passed your house about twenty minutes ago. I saw the antenna on your roof, and, being a ham myself, I couldn't resist walking down to meet you."

"Come right in," I told him. "My husband is sleeping, but you're welcome to see our station."

"You have fine equipment," he said, as he stepped into the radio room, his eyes wide with excitement.

"My husband built it himself," I told him, proudly.

"Where are your from?" I asked. "This is a new experience for me; to meet a ham from another country."

He smiled, then said, "I'm German. I know my Yankee accent may be confusing, but I learned to speak English as a prisoner-of-war on an American ship. It was months before we made port. I was anxious to learn the language, and they were kind enough to teach me. "Someday," he added, wistfully, "I hope to have a radio station just like this."

Well, over the years I had met Canadian- and American-Germans, but for the first time I was face to face with a German-German. I liked him!

Bill Korff was the first of hundreds of visitors from foreign lands. The short-wave antenna on our roof was a symbol of international brotherhood; the welcome sign to all hams. Our knowledge of the world about us and our interest in people from all countries increased with every contact we made.

One day came sailors from a Norwegian ship of the Fjell-Oranje Line. They laughed when I said, "We call your ships Orange Jelly!"

One day, on my radio I heard a British soldier from a station in Iraq. Here was a new country. I gave him a call. No answer. It seemed that every ham on the air wanted to talk to him. "Oh, boy!" I thought, "This will be easy. Once he hears my female voice, he's bound to answer." Well, that was once I was wrong. I called and called for hours. Day after day, I tried to get him. Finally, I had to admit defeat. "Woman hater!" I told Cy, in disgust.

Weeks later, when talking to some airmen on Malta, another station broke into our conversation. "This is Iraq calling VE3DTW." I couldn't believe my ears. Here was the station I had tried to get for such a long time.

"This is wonderful!" I told him. "You'll never know how many times I called your station.

"Sorry, Ethel," he answered. "This is the first time I've heard you." It seems that so many were calling him at the same time, it just created a cacophony of sound, and he was unable at times to distinguish one call from another.

When I told Cy about this, he roared laughing. "This is just what you needed, honey," he said. "You were so sure it was your voice that brought all the choice calls your way . . . now you know it takes a good strong signal from a high-powered station." I knew he was right.

Soon I was adding more countries to my list — Madagascar, Ifni, Tierra del Fuego, Fiji, Hawaii, and many others. Then, one day I heard another girl on the air. I called her.

"This is W6UHA, Maxine Willis, California," she said. "I've been licensed for five years, but have just come on phone."

Then she told me she had been listening to me on the air, and hoped we would become good friends. From that day on, Maxine and I have been like sisters. We have so many things in common, it seems uncanny. We enjoy weekly schedules for chats, which often last over an hour. After the war, Maxine carried messages for American servicemen stationed in Japan, the same way I did for our Canadian boys overseas. We have a mutual respect and admiration for each other that is not too often found between women.

After Maxine, more and more women came on phone. I became friendly with several girls in England, and then I met Louise, PAO ZC. Louise Ten Herkel was born in Montreal. Her family moved to Holland when she was a girl. There, she married Hans, a dentist, and, just before the war started, they had a little boy. The German occupation was very hard on them, and when the war ended, they came to Canada, where Hans took a post-graduate course at McGill University. Back in The Netherlands, Hans opened an office in The Hague. He encouraged Louise to join him in his hobby, ham radio, and she became the first YL (Young Lady) ham in Holland.

"I am so happy to know you, Ethel," she told me. "I loved Canada, and I would like to have a schedule to talk to you every week. Would that suit you?"

"I'd love it," I assured her, and from that day on our weekly chats became something very special to both of us.

Everyone in ham radio is known by his radio call and his given name. Controversial subjects, religion and politics are never discussed. Profanity and vulgar language are forbidden, and monitor stations are on the alert for any breaches in this code of ethics.

Romance can bloom over the airwaves. I became very annoyed by one young man who insisted on calling me endearing names. When he said, "Ethel, your signal is so clear this morning, I can hear your heartbeat," I told another ham friend that I refused to speak to him again.

"Oh, don't do that," he said. "I'll drop you a note in the mail, and you'll understand."

A couple of days later, his letter came, telling me that my amorous friend was in fact a hopeless cripple, confined to a wheelchair. "Ham radio is his only lifeline to the outside world," he wrote. "Let him enjoy his little masquerade. It can't do you any harm."

Not long after that I missed him on the air. I learned that he had died.

Thousands of handicapped people find ham radio the answer to their prayers for a fuller, more useful life. Because they can spend their hours simply listening-in, they are often able to alert other hams to signals of distress, such as SOS at sea.

Men on isolated weather stations, prospectors and bush pilots can keep in touch with those at home by ham radio. I have spent many happy hours chatting with these lonely fellows.

Radio operators on ships, "Sparks," are always an interesting source of converstion. They love to talk with someone ashore, especially when they are thousands of miles from home. I like hearing about their voyages to all the corners of the world. One day a ship's captain asked me to contact his wife by phone, collect.

"I've been at sea for six months," he said. "We dock in New York, next Friday, and I have two weeks' leave. I want to take her to Florida for a holiday. I'll make reservations at a good hotel, and we'll have –" He hesitated a few moments, then said, "we'll have a second honeymoon."

Well, being romantic myself, I was anxious to call his wife, but I had to tell him that we had no phone. He sounded so letdown, I just had to find a way to get in touch with his wife. I said, "If you keep your receiver on my frequency, I'll drive to the canal office and make the long distance call from there. I'll be back as soon as possible with her answer." He gave me her name and phone number, and I, happy to play Cupid, jumped into the car, and drove through heavy rain to the mainland office. The operator got the captain's wife, who at first refused to accept the call.

"I'm an amateur radio operator," I explained. "I've just been talking to your husband over the air. He asked me to give you this message." I then told her of her husband's proposal.

Well, I've never heard anything in my life like her lame excuses. First of all, she pretended she couldn't hear a word I said. The long-distance operator offered to relay the message. Finally the wife answered, with a few well-chosen words, denouncing her husband, then she added, "Tell him I have a cold. I'm in no condition to travel, and furthermore, I have no intention of meeting him in New York. If he wants to see me he can come home to Philadelphia!" She hung up!

I was stunned. The operator was just as shocked as I.

"What will you tell the poor man?" she asked.

"Oh, I'll think of something," I assured her. On the way home I pondered over what I could say. How could I tell him the truth? . . . not in front of his men! When I called his ship's radio I had made up my mind. "Your wife is very sorry, but she has a bad cold. She thinks it would be unwise for her to travel at this time," I told him. Then, sensing his disappointment, I couldn't help telling a lie. "She sends you all her love!" Maybe that would soften the blow, for, after all, radio messages are anything but private. There is always someone listening-in.

One day when I was talking to Jack, G3FJ, in Slough, England, he said, "King George and Queen Elizabeth will visit our city tomorrow. The streets are gay with flags, and everyone's excited."

I told him I was surprised at this, since Windsor Castle is so near his home, and I thought seeing the Royal Family might be commonplace. Then I told him about the Royal Visit to Canada in 1939.

"Their Majesties were going to ride through St. Catharines, following a parade of school children, veterans and dignitaries. It was the first time our city had ever had this honour. A holiday was declared, and thousands of people lined the streets, taking along stools and chairs for the long wait. What excitement! My heart nearly burst with pride when they drove by. King George was wearing his naval uniform, his face very tanned and handsome. The Queen looked like a beautiful Dresden doll in powder blue hat and gown, and holding a frilly blue parasol. She sat beside her husband, in an open convertible car, waving to the crowds, so gracious, smiling and completely captivating.

"They were escorted on a leisurely drive along the Lakeshore Road and the Niagara River to Queenston Heights, thence over the Niagara Bridge to New York State, where they would board a special train to New York City. Cy and I jumped into our car and raced ahead to Queenston Heights, so we could get another good look at the pair. Sure enough, along they came, still smiling gaily at the crowds. Having the rest of the day off, we drove across the river to Niagara Falls, New York, and had supper, then went to a movie. It was 11 p.m. when we left the show, and found everyone running in the direction of the railway station. We ran, too.

"It's the Royal Train! " everyone was yelling.

Cy, about to climb Main Light tower.

Cy, checking Main Light.

"One by one the coaches slowly rolled by, blinds tightly drawn. It was well past 11 o'clock; they must be asleep, after such a strenuous day. Still we watched, holding in our disappointment, as the last coach began passing by; then, suddenly there arose a wild, spontaneous cheer. There stood our Queen, alone on the platform; still smiling, still waving, still beautiful! A wave of emotion crept over me. Pride? Admiration of her courage? I can't explain. But, on glancing around at the crowd, through my tears, I saw the same emotion had touched them all. There wasn't a dry eye amongst them!"

As I reached this part of my story, I was actually reliving my emotions. I couldn't speak.

Cy took the mike from my hands and said, "You'll have to excuse Ethel, Jack. She's crying."

"Never mind," said Jack, "She's got me crying too!"

Just then another ham, Ron, G2CDI, broke into the conversation, "You're not the only one!" he announced.

I couldn't help wondering, "What is this mystical bond?"

Not all messages are of a personal nature. Most countries encourage ham radio, for the operators are a ready-trained group of dedicated people who can be called upon in any emergency. In times of disaster, forest fires, floods and illness, hams have worked around the clock relaying messages and instructions to the Red Cross and others, and sending reports to anxious relatives.

When telephone lines are down, if there is a ham operator nearby, messages can be sent immediately. Sometimes a radio message goes halfway around the world before it reaches its destination. Short-wave listeners often share in this mission by relaying messages by telephone.

Each major country has a representative group or groups of amateurs dedicated to promoting this fascinating hobby and helping fellow hams. The

ARRL (Amateur Radio Relay League) has many members in the United States and Canada. The RSGB (Radio Society of Great Britain) is the British group, and the Central Radio Club of Moscow is the Russian. These groups encourage good fellowship, high standards of operating, and self-censorship. These Societies and many more are dedicated to furthering understanding and friendship between all nations.

A small group of women had been involved in amateur radio experiments from the beginning, but it wasn't until 1939 that a few girl operators, including Ethel Pick of Montreal, got together and formed a womans' group called Young Ladies' Radio League, YLRL. This organization includes licensed female operators from all over the world, and I was proud to have been invited to become the District Representative of all Canada.

I now had so many schedules with radio friends that the day didn't seem to have enough hours. I would rush through my housework, then spend an hour talking to Maxine in California, Louise in Wassenaar, Margaret and Jack in London or Ida in Chile.

Foreign countries on amateur radio are known as DX. By this time Doug and Bruce were calling me DX MAMA! I must hasten to add I didn't neglect my family. My men would never have allowed that. Cy was just as keen as I about my interest in radio. Every distant station I contacted was really a feather in his cap for it was really his handiwork, his equipment and his encouragement that made it possible.

Never again would I be lonely. All I had to do was flick a switch and I could talk to friends in a dozen countries. All that plus a loving husband and two healthy, home-loving sons! What more could a woman wish for?

"South American" Cruise ship.

Chapter Twelve
PROBLEMS AND SOLUTIONS

The months slipped by. It was now mid December, 1946. The last saltie had sailed past our lighthouse, heading for Montreal and the open sea. The weather was damp and cold. Our old electric heaters were useless. Cy bought the largest Quebec heater (coal stove) he could find and set it up in the middle of our living room. The warmth of the coal fire was welcome beyond belief. Our evenings were spent cuddled close to the stove, reading, helping the boys with homework, and singing oldtime songs. Cy built a recorder, and we made silly records, then played them back amidst gales of laughter.

Now came the last-minute rush of lake shipping before the winter freeze-up. Already there was a thin sheet of ice on the canal. Through long narrow cracks in the ice, cold grey water shimmered jelly-like in the sun. Hundreds of ducks floated lazily in these open places, half-asleep, their black heads tucked into their white breasts, looking to me like giant sprays of full-blown pussy willows.

The canal closed officially on the 23rd of December. The boys could hardly wait to move back to town, but many chores had to be done first. Water must be drained from all the pipes, and coal oil poured down the toilet and all drains to keep them from freezing. Finally our furniture was loaded into a moving van; venetian blinds closed, and all windows and doors locked and bolted; and, with deep sighs of relief we headed for our home in the city.

We had a wonderful Christmas, but, strangely enough, once the Yuletide season was ended, we began to miss the peace and quiet of the lighthouse. City noises, salesmen knocking at the door and the constant ringing of the telephone really bothered us. Doug and Bruce filled their free time with skating, hockey games and all the activities they had missed. They grumbled a little when Cy told them we'd decided to return to the lighthouse by the middle of March. "I want to overhaul the radio beacon before the canal opens," he explained, "and Mother and I would like to make some alterations in the house."

We hadn't counted on a heavy March snowstorm on our moving day. Cy had gone to the lighthouse earlier in the day to light the Quebec heater so the house had warmed up considerably. What a mess the movers made of our floors! By the time the furniture was arranged and the dishes unpacked, I was a wreck. This had been our third moving in a year and I had had it! "I don't care if we freeze to death," I declared, "I'm through with all this moving!"

"I agree," said Cy. "This is murder. Maybe we can do something to this place to make it liveable in the winter. We could get storm windows; maybe an oil space heater."

"Could a furnace be installed?" I asked. Cy shook his head.

"It would cost a fortune. However, maybe one day the government will decide to do that. The ceilings are so darn high. That's where most of our heat goes. They could be lowered, y'know. Oh, there are so many things that could be done to make the place comfortable."

Cy's words were encouraging. Maybe we could avoid these dreadful movings. Meanwhile, we must get busy. There were so many things to do before the opening of navigation.

The following day the snow had melted and Cy went out to inspect the main light tower. A few minutes later he came into the kitchen. He was furious. "Vandals have broken into the tower room, tipped all the mercury out, smashed the light bulbs and just about ruined the place! What pleasure could anyone get out of doing such a wicked thing?" He shook his fist. "Boy!" he said, gritting his teeth, and his eyes wild with anger, "I'd like to get my hands on the guys who did that!" I shuddered at the thought of what he could do when aroused and I was secretly thankful that he didn't know.

When the boys came home from school this was the topic of conversation. "Who would do such a wicked thing?" I asked.

"I bet I know," said Doug, "the beach boys; sure as fate, it was them."

"Who do you mean, Doug?" asked Cy. "Do we know them?"

"Remember last fall, Dad? Remember those tough-looking guys in that old beat-up truck? You caught them at the end of the pier picking up driftwood. You didn't like their looks, and ordered them to stay away and never come back. They said they had always collected firewood along the pier. You said they could do what they wanted on the rest of the piers but they mustn't come past the lighthouse."

"Yes," said Cy, "they were sure a scruffy-looking lot; only kids, too. I wondered why they weren't in school."

"Well, Dad, it's not all their fault. They live in a shack near the beach. They have no father, and their mother runs a bootleg place; y'know, where people can buy beer on Sunday. She's always being arrested by the police, but she keeps on doing it."

"How come you know so much about them?" asked Cy.

"Oh, everyone knows about them at the beach." Doug looked at Bruce, who nodded his head.

"Sure, Dad," he said. "We always see them over there when we hike to the hot dog stand at the beach. They're always somewhere around. They sure have a bad name. Why, once a little launch drifted away from its mooring and washed up on the beach. Those guys had it stripped so fast, no one had a chance to stop them!"

"I'm going right over to the beach and bang their heads together!"

"Gee, Dad, I'd be afraid to tangle with them. They're tough, — real tough. They'd only keep on doing mean tricks on us. We'd never know what they might do next." Cy thought it over for a few minutes.

"I know what," he said, "I have a plan. Don't know if it'll work but it's worth a try. The next time I see them gathering wood, I'll tell them someone broke into government property and did a lot of damage. I'll pretend I haven't a clue about the guilty parties, but if they'll keep a lookout for me in future, they can have all the driftwood they want. What do you fellows think? Will they fall for it?"

"It's worth trying, Dad," said Doug. "I don't think we'll have any more trouble if you put them on their honour. I think the reason they're so bad is because everyone's against them; they've never been given a break."

A couple of days later Cy saw the boys with their old truck. He felt like giving them a real walloping, but, holding in his natural impulse, he pretended he was asking for their help in locating the vandals who had broken into government property. "You boys are around here a lot," he said, "If you keep an eye on the place for me, you can collect all the wood you want."

It really worked! In all the years we have been here, there was never another break-in! They proved themselves on at least one other occasion.

Doug had been allowed to take the car to town one Saturday afternoon, so he and Bruce could attend a movie. On the way home on the canal road the car swerved into a soft clay shoulder. The more Doug spun the wheels, the deeper he went into the rut. The beach boys were nearby. They tied our car to their truck and pulled it free.

Long before the ice had disappeared from the canal, the smelt were running. Hundreds of fishermen lined the canal banks, lifting bushels of little fish in their nets. I made a net from an old lace curtain and a wire hoop, and the boys went out on the dock to try their luck. When they came in with over a hundred smelt, I couldn't believe my eyes.

"Can we have some for supper?" they asked, "They're supposed to be delicious." I nodded my head and smiled.

"I've never cooked smelt before," I told them, "but I'll try."

Cy and the boys cleaned them and I fried two big panfuls. I made a tossed green salad to go with them, and we really went to town. We ate until our tummies could hold no more. It was really delicious, but I've never been tempted to fry a mess of smelt since that day.

The canal opened on schedule, and soon the ships were sailing to and fro. It was like greeting old friends when we recognized ships from the year before. The beautiful, white passenger ships — Noranda and the South American sailed past, their decks crowded with happy vacationers headed for a tour of the Thousand Islands or some other fascinating place. I used to daydream of the things they would see on their cruise. Then came the giant lakers, headed by that old stalwart, Lemoyne, the giant carrier — 633 feet long — which officially opened the Welland Canal in 1932.

One day a group of workmen arrived. "We're going to put up two new buildings at the pierhead," they told Cy. The government had ordered a concrete building to house the generators and a new foghorn, and a wooden building for two new transmitters for the radio beacon. There would also be a new steel tower adjacent to the radio building. This would be a modern antenna for the beacon.

"Oh, Cy," I exclaimed, as soon as the men left for the pierhead, "won't it be wonderful to be rid of those noisy generators!" Cy smiled in agreement.

"I'm going to make you a really nice kitchen, honey. The little kitchen will be fine for the boys' bedroom, and this Watchroom is the largest room in the house. I'll make built-in cupboards all down one side of the room. We'll have the 'fridge, stove and sink all nearby. The other side of the room will be our dining area. How would you like a new dining suite?" I clapped my hands in glee.

"That would be marvellous!" I exclaimed. "Oh, it's going to be so much fun."

"It's going to be lots of work, first, honey. I'll have to get some of the canal workers to help me move these concrete slabs. We'll need hydraulic drills to do that job. I'll do all the woodwork. I'll need some help from you later on, dear. Make sure we have lots of dust covers for the furniture. That concrete raises an awful lot of dust."

The next few weeks were busy ones for us. What a transformation in our home. The boys now had a real bedroom, and my kitchen was a dream. We painted the woodwork white, and papered the dining area walls with pink, white and pale green striped wallpaper. Our new maple set looked elegant, and the windows had frilly white curtains, parted to show a row of pink geraniums on the window sill.

The buildings and tower were finally finished, and the new equipment was ready to install. Cy wanted to do this himself, then he would be better qualified to make repairs if anything went wrong.

Canal electricians put up new heavier-type wiring, all the new machines and transmitters would be operated by remote control from a panel of switches and clocks inside our house. Several battery alarms were installed to warn us of trouble or breakdown in the equipment.

That summer was so busy for all of us that the fall came before we realized it. Our first indication of the coming cold weather was the arrival of storm windows. Cy had ordered them from the Lighthouse Department of stores in Prescott, and we were delighted to see them. We had bought a large space oil heater, and now we were ready to face the coming winter. The canal people had promised to keep the road clear of snow. This was progress. Another happy note was a go-ahead sign for Cy to ask for bids to dig a deep well. The future looked much brighter.

Several times during the winter we had questioned Doug about his plans for college. He would graduate from high school the next June and he was still undecided about the future. He had talked of going to Royal Roads Naval Academy, for he loved being in Sea Cadets. We went along with him on that, but, as he neared graduation, he changed his mind. He just wouldn't discuss it. Because he was an excellent scholar, both Cy and I were anxious for him to further his education. We worried about it a great deal.

Finally, after a heart-to-heart talk, he admitted a reluctance to go to college. "I hated high school," he said, "maybe because I was younger than the other boys. I don't know. All I do know is that I would like to find a job; a position of trust; something where I would be assured of advancement."

"What about banking?" Cy suggested.

"That would probably be the answer," Doug said. "I don't know, really I don't."

"Well," said Cy, "at least we have something to work on. How would you like me to talk to Mr. Mackenzie at the Royal Bank tomorrow? I'll ask his advice. He's been our bank manager for years; he knows you and our circumstances; I'm sure he'd be the best person to ask."

Cy had an interview with Mr. Mackenzie the next morning.

"We had always planned for Doug to go to college," Cy told him, "but Doug is such a serious-minded boy, when he says he doesn't want to go, I know he really means it. I'm not going to insist unless you think it is absolutely necessary."

"Well," said Mr. Mackenzie, "the bank has never needed young men as urgently as it does right now. Many of our young men who went into the Service were lost to us; some were killed; others chose to go into other lines of business. I can assure you, Mr. Williamson, if your son joins the bank now, it will be to his advantage." Mr. Mackenzie also told Cy about college courses offered by the bank which would be available to Doug in the future.

That was how our elder son became a banker. A tall, earnest young man with a handsome face, good manners and a pleasing personality, he certainly looked the part.

Bruce was now attending high school, but oh, what a difference there is in brothers! School for Bruce was a wonderful place for fun and sports. He played everything from hockey to lacrosse, and loved every minute of it. He never tried to excel in either school work or sports; that would have ruined the fun. He had friends by the dozens. He was slightly shorter than Doug, slim and fair, with a sunny disposition and a "don't care" attitude about his clothes. Although we worried about his carefree ways, we all agreed Bruce was a joy to have around.

Transportation was still a problem for the boys. Now that Doug was working, he went to town and came home at different hours than Bruce. He decided to buy a small motorcycle. There was no heavy traffic between the lighthouse and town in those days so the motor bike was a fine idea. On rainy days he wore a shower-proof jacket but his trousers got wet. I made him a pair of black leatherette chaps with elastic bands at the back. He slipped these on over his trousers and they kept him dry. Later on he bought a used car.

Doug found his work fascinating. He began to dress and act the way he thought a banker should. This sometimes was carried to extremes, and we secretly enjoyed many a laugh at his expense. For one thing, he found Cy's black derby hat in an old hatbox. This hadn't been in style for over twenty years but, because the Mayor of the city wore one, and always looked distinguished, our Doug decided to wear his father's.

"Never mind, Doug," the chief accountant told him one day when some of the bank staff were teasing him, "wear your hat. It becomes you. When you walk down the street everyone will say 'There goes Mr. Williamson!' "

He wore his derby on his first holiday in New York City. He travelled alone, by bus, and had a fine time seeing all the sights from the Statue of Liberty to the Latin Quarter.

I had arranged to meet his bus in Buffalo but was half-an-hour late. He was waiting in front of the bus terminal and greeted me with a big smile. "Hi, Mom!" he said, giving me a big hug and kiss. He put his bag into the car trunk, then took my place behind the wheel. "New York is really something," he said, as we moved along the highway towards home.

"How did you make out with your hat?" I asked with a broad grin. I had noticed he was still wearing it with a jaunty air.

"Nobody even noticed it in New York," he said, "but, coming home on the bus, it caused quite a stir. Two girls sitting behind me had an argument. One said I must be an undertaker; the other girl insisted I was a politician! They couldn't see me laughing, and neither of them had the courage to ask me."

"That must have been funny!" I said. "We all thought you would have thrown it away and bought a new hat to wear."

"Never!" he said, sharply. "I love it and I don't care what people think." We had just crossed the Peace Bridge over the Niagara River when he said, "I must tell you the funniest thing about the hat. It was while I was waiting for you in front of the terminal. A cab driver stopped a couple of times to ask if I wanted a ride. 'My car's coming for me,' I told him. Finally, curiosity got the best of him. He leaned out of his cab, and, in a loud whisper, said, 'Confidentially, Bud, what the hell racket are you in?' "

At supper that night, Doug had us in fits of laughter as he told us of his adventures in New York. Later, when Cy and I were alone, we were chatting about the boys; Doug in particular.

"Isn't it a good thing," I said, "that in spite of Doug's rather dogmatic ideas, he can still laugh at himself?" Cy agreed.

It was now late fall. Very few cars ventured down our pier. The only visitors we had were what we called our "foul weather friends," Graham and Belle Peacock. Graham was a pharmacist and, like Cy, an oldtime radio ham. Belle and I had many things in common and we enjoyed each other's company.

I now spent more and more time chatting over the air. One Saturday morning, during a regular schedule with an English friend, Ron Plant, I had a pleasant surprise. "Ethel," he said, "a mobile unit of the British Broadcasting Company is ready and waiting to record a Christmas message from your lighthouse. If we allow you a few minutes to think it over, will you be kind enough to give us a ten minute talk on how you intend to spend a Canadian Christmas in your home at the Lighthouse?"

59

This came like a bombshell! Never before had I done such a thing. Why, I used to get sick when I had to recite poetry at school! How could I do this? Beads of perspiration ran down my face and I was trembling all over. I had to make a quick decision. "Y--Yes," I said, then began scribbling notes at random, for there wasn't much time. Cy stood by, grinning like a Cheshire cat.

"I wouldn't want to be you for all the money in the world!" he announced, shaking his head and raising both hands in mock horror.

When I called Ron, I knew that every word would be recorded. Trying to keep my voice calm and natural, I talked about our lighthouse and the canal; the freighters and foreign ships that sailed by; the woods surrounding our house on the pier; and the Christmas cake I had just made. I tried to give him a word picture of a Canadian Christmas. When it was over, I was wet and limp with nervous exhaustion.

"It came over perfectly," said Ron. "Now we'll play it back so you can hear it." I couldn't believe it was my own voice I was listening to. It was so clear; no trace of fear or nerves. Thank goodness it hadn't been television! Ron then told me my message would be broadcast all over Britain on Christmas Day.

About one week before the closing of navigation we had an early sleet storm. The boys were in bed and Cy and I were enjoying a cup of tea.

"I hope nothing goes wrong tonight," said Cy, with a shudder. I winced at the idea, for a thick coating of ice already covered the trees and buildings. Cy donned a jacket and went outside to check the lights. "Well," he announced, "that's what I get for opening my big mouth. The main light's out!"

This had been our greatest fear ever since coming to the lighthouse. There was only one thing to do; climb that tower; up 150 steps and make repairs, immediately! This time the steel steps and handrails would be coated with ice.

"Oh, no!" I cried, in alarm. "You can't go." Cy turned as he went out the door and smiled wryly.

"Say one of your little prayers, honey," he said. "They seem to work!"

Through the bedroom window I watched him start up the steps, his toolbag slung over his shoulder, while he hung onto the rails with both hands. I dropped to my knees, whispering over and over, "Please, God, keep him safe . . . oh, please keep him safe."

He'd been gone, oh, such a long time! I couldn't stay inside any longer. Putting on my coat and a kerchief, I ventured outside; picking my way over the icy ground to the foot of the tower. I strained to see through the sleety rain, but it was impossible to make anything out of the darkness. I thought I saw the flicker of an oil lamp through the tiny window, above, but I couldn't be sure. I thought of our sons sleeping soundly in the house. It was just as well they slept. They couldn't have helped any more than I. Suddenly I heard a door slam. It must be the trap door above.

"Are you all right, dear?" I called out.

"What the heck are you doing out here?" he yelled. "Sure I'm all right. I'll be with you in a minute." Silently he made his way down the steps. I clutched his arm as he reached the ground, and we slithered over the ice to the house. My eyes were smarting with tears, and I silently whispered, "Thank God." Later, I said, "I hope that never happens again."

"It's all in a day's work," he said, but he did admit it was a frightening experience. "I'm going to hook the light to an alarm bell," he told me. "Then we'll know immediately if the light burns out."

From the window we watched the long beam swing over the lake, guiding the ships through the storm.

Chapter Thirteen
CALIFORNIA HERE WE COME!

After nine months of continuous duty at the lighthouse we really looked forward to a three-month winter vacation. We were excitedly awaiting the closing of navigation this year for we had made plans early in the spring, and were prepared for a special treat.

During his visit to the lighthouse, Ivan, Cy's brother, had asked, "Why don't you build a house trailer, Cy? You could spend your winter holidays with us in California."

We thought this was a wonderful idea. Cy bought a chassis and wheels, then he and the boys spent every spare moment of the summer building our trailer. It wasn't finished until the day before Christmas, but it was a beauty, complete with oil heater, cook stove and refrigerator.

It had been a terrific project, taking months of labour, but, knowing the thrilling reward waiting for us at the end, we all worked cheerfully to make it the finest house-trailer possible.

Doug had arranged for a month's vacation from the bank, and Bruce had asked at school for an extension of his Christmas holidays.

All Christmas week we packed bags, and loaded the trailer with groceries, dishes and cooking utensils. Money restrictions were still in effect; we were allowed but one hundred dollars each to take out of Canada.

Many last minute chores had to be done at the lighthouse. Everything that might be carried away by thieves must be stored inside the house. Even the rowboat had to be hauled into the kitchen. Special locks were put on the tower light and on all doors, and we arranged for a short term insurance to cover any losses.

By New Year's Eve we were ready. I was placing pots of geraniums in a large galvanized tub on the kitchen floor. Maybe if I left them in a couple of inches of water, they would survive. An electric heater nearby would keep them from freezing.

"The radio announcer says we're going to have a heavy snowstorm to-night," Doug announced from his bedroom.

"It's started already," said Bruce, looking through the window. Then, seeing alarm in my face, he added, "Don't worry, Mom. We'll get you out. After all, you have three men!"

"Yes," I thought; then closed my eyes: "Thank God for that!"

"We'll have to get up about 5 o'clock," said Cy. "Maybe we'll get out before it piles up too much. The only job left will be to drain the water pipes."

We went to bed at last, but none of us slept well. The moment the alarm rang, we were up. I ran to the window, then called, "Hurry, boys, it's beginning to drift already!" I dashed to the stove and started to prepare breakfast.

"Thank Goodness we've got chains for the tires!" said Cy, peering through the window at the swirling snow. "We'll be lucky if we get out. There won't be any snowplow today, with it being a holiday. All the men are off work today."

Doug was dressed. He started making toast over the stove burner. (Our toaster was packed for the trip.)

"I can't get Toronto on the radio, Dad," said Bruce, "but I just heard that Buffalo is snowed in. It's the worst storm in years."

"It doesn't seem too bad here," said Cy. "I'm sure if we can make it up the canal road, we'll be all set. At least we know the main highways will be cleared. Let's hurry; that's the best we can do."

Half an hour later, chains on the tires and a snow shovel tied to the back of the car, we began our trip to California. A hundred yards up the road we hit our first snowdrift, about three feet high. "Here goes!" cried Cy, as we made a dash through it. Snow flew like a blinding sheet, but we made it. Strong winds had swept parts of the road clean, but where there were drifts, it was tough going.

At last we came to the gates leading to the highway. Here was the highest drift of all. Cy and the boys took turns with the shovel. After about half an hour's digging, they tried to push the car while I stepped on the gas. We couldn't budge it!

"I guess we're the first ones out this morning." said Bruce. Sure enough; there wasn't a blemish on the snow. It was already seven o'clock. There must be some snowplows at work. We wrapped ourselves in blankets and settled in our seats for a long wait.

Everything was so still; so crisp and pristine white. The snowfall had stopped, and it looked as if God had laid a starched, white linen tablecloth over the land. There wasn't even the sound of a bird. The world looked so beautiful, a lump came into my throat. My eyes filled with tears, as I turned to my menfolk. "This must be as the world looked on the very first day," I murmured.

Just then, Cy stepped out of the car. "I'll have a look down the road," he said. "I might see a snowplow."

Suddenly, a gust of wind whipped off his fedora hat and sent it wheeling off on top of the snow! He started after it, every step past his knees in snow. He looked so funny; this giant of a man chasing a hat; I began to laugh. The boys joined me, and when Cy finally returned, with his hat, we tried to stop, but couldn't.

Instead of being angry, he saw the joke, and laughed with us.

Moments later, a plow came along, and we followed in its path, until I spotted a mailbox, at the side of the road.

"Will you stop dear," I said. "I'd like to post some letters."

"Oh, no!" Cy shouted, "not at a time like this!"

"I'm sorry, dear, but they are cheques; important cheques that must be in the mail." The car stopped, and I was out before the boys had a chance to move. I took four ostrich-like steps towards the mailbox, and, suddenly dropped waist-deep into a snowfilled ditch! Now it was Cy's turn to laugh at me. The air was filled with howls of merriment. I was furious. Then, realizing the spectacle I'd made of myself, I had to laugh with them.

Cy jumped out of the car; grabbed me under the arms and hauled me up onto the cleared roadway. "Oh, dear!" I cried, "Why didn't I wear slacks?" I could feel the cold snow right up to my armpits. Cy brushed off as much as he could, as I stamped and shook myself. Luckily, the car was nice and warm. I dried out eventually.

We followed snowplows all the way to London, Ontario. From there on we had no more snow. I was assigned the job of navigator, and the fellows took turns driving.

We had lunch in Windsor, then crossed the bridge into Detroit, Michigan. I pointed to Route 24, but, in the busy New Year's traffic, I missed one of the signs. We finally hit the highway again, and began to make headway. I must have dozed for a while, for suddenly, I screamed out, "Something's wrong!"

"What's wrong?" the three fellows cried.

"The sun is setting on the wrong side of the car!"

"I don't get it," said Cy, braking, and stopping quickly. They all looked at me as if I were crazy.

"Well," I explained, "we're supposed to be driving south; the sun should set on our right. It isn't. It's on our left!"

Groans of disgust came from the three fellows, and no wonder; for we had travelled more than sixty-five miles in the wrong direction! We had to turn around and drive all the way back through heavy holiday traffic. Finally, just a few miles south of Detroit, we decided we'd had enough driving for one day. We found a small clearing beside the highway, and stopped for the night.

"What a navigator!" teased Doug. That phrase was to ring in my ears for the entire trip. I felt badly, but other incidents occurred later, and we just tried to make fun of the whole thing. This was our first family vacation since before the war, and, as the boys were nearly young men, it very likely could be the last one we could have together. We would make it a memorable holiday.

With three drivers, the journey was very pleasant. Things went smoothly until we neared Indianapolis, Indiana. Then, a blow-out! It was a new tire on the trailer. We were nearby a service station, and luckily, we had a Credit Card, for our American funds were limited. The garage man told us that our trailer was too heavy for the type of tires we had. He insisted on changing them for larger ones with a heavier tread. Thus equipped, we gaily went on our way. Once we had passed through the big city, we were able to speed up on the highway, then, we smelled burning rubber!

We pulled off the road into a little trailer park, and all got out to investigate. Well — it seemed that our new tires were too large for the tire-wells Cy had made in the trailer. Every revolution of the wheels had caused friction, and when we finally got rolling along the highway, the heat from the friction had caused rubber shavings to melt, and we found great globs of melted rubber inside the tire-wells.

"We've had it!" announced Cy. "We can't go on like this. I guess we'll have to leave the trailer here and go on without it."

Cy went into the caretaker's office; told him of our predicament, and made arrangements to leave the trailer in the park until our return from California. We gave him $15 to cover expenses, then, after a good night's sleep, we transferred all the perishable food, the toaster and electric tea kettle to the car; locked the windows and doors of the trailer and, not without mixed feelings of regret and relief, continued on our way to California.

We found Highway 66 at St. Louis, and from there on we had no problems. We were excited about seeing all the noted places along the way; Indian families, adobe houses, the Painted Desert and the marvellous Grand Canyon, but sad to say, it was the thousands and thousands of empty, rusted beer cans on each side of the highway, that left the biggest impression. There just wasn't a clear space to make a picnic, for hundreds of miles!

The desert land proved disappointing to me. Instead of miles of golden, rippled sand, there was nothing but dirt and scrubland. Then came the cactus, in all shapes and sizes. This was a new experience. I reached out to touch one, and for the next two hours, I was kept busy, removing tiny hair-like prickles from my hand.

We loved the mountains. Never had we seen such awe-inspiring peaks and chasms. It was frightening, too, as we came into California, at Needles. The perilous turns on the mountain road, and the view below from that great height, were enough to make anyone nervous.

"California has just got to be worth all this!" I declared. "Otherwise, how did the pioneers ever have the courage to continue?" Well, it wasn't long before we were aware of the lush beauty, the magnificent grandeur of this semi-tropical Paradise. As yet there were no freeways, nor the vast numbers of cars that are there today. Oh, Los Angeles was a great metropolis, but the suburbs were a quiet, delightful refuge from the rush and strain of big city traffic.

Ivan and Margot lived in Glendale, in the San Fernando Valley. In those days, it was like being in a pleasant small town. We loved each street, lined with different varieties of trees; the evergreens, the mountains in the background, and the beautiful flowers. The weather? It was delightful, warm and sunny. It seemed unbelievable that we had left all that ice and snow just one week ago.

I was anxious to meet my radio friend, Maxine. At last I found a chance to phone her. She knew my voice right away.

"Oh, Ethel," she said, "we must get together soon. Our Los Angeles Young Ladies' Radio Club meets tomorrow afternoon. We would love to have you. Bring Cy, too, for we're having a male speaker. I'm sure he'll be happier with another man in the room."

Then she added, "Come early, Ethel. That'll give us a chance to get acquainted before the crowd arrives." She gave me the address of the YWCA on Figueroa Street.

I could hardly wait for the time to pass until noon the next day. After an early lunch, we drove to downtown Los Angeles. I rushed Cy into the "Y" at least twenty minutes before the time we had arranged for our meeting.

Well, we waited and waited. No Maxine. By 2 o'clock all other members of the club had arrived. We introduced ourselves, and they assured us that Maxine would be there, for she had told them we were coming. We met the guest speaker, and the program commenced. Still no Maxine. By this time, in spite of the friendliness of the group, I was feeling embarrassed and upset. How could she do this to me? At four o'clock, when a lunch was about to be served, we had given up hope of meeting Maxine; then in she came!

All eyes turned to her, and everyone exclaimed, "Maxine!" They all wanted to know what had happened, but she came directly towards Cy and me. She was about my height, 5'2", and very slim. Her chestnut brown hair was cut short, with bangs, like Claudette Colbert's, and it curled softly around her face. She looked very feminine and dainty, and had a lovely warm smile.

"Will you ever forgive me?" she pleaded. Then she explained what had happened. "I was so nervous about our meeting," she said, "that I got sick to my stomach." She paused. "Then, I broke out in hives! — I called my doctor, and told him I had to attend this meeting. He advised me against it, but, when I insisted, he gave me a sedative. I daren't drive, after that, so I had to come by bus."

We sat together to have some coffee and sandwiches, and it wasn't until I removed my new black kid gloves that I realized my own emotions at our meeting. My hands were dyed black with perspiration! I went to the washroom and tried to wash them clean but it made hardly any impression. (It took nearly a week for me to get rid of that black stain.)

Well, after that most embarrassing get-together, we couldn't help but relax and really get to know each other. We insisted on driving Maxine to her home where we met her husband, Ed. We learned that Ed Willis was an oldtime ham of great reputation, for he held the honour of being the first radio operator to send a message on 20 metres from the West Coast to the East Coast of the U.S.

Ed was a sound technician at Metro Goldwyn-Mayer Studios. He had been a personal friend of Mary Pickford and Douglas Fairbanks in the old days. We spent a wonderful evening with our radio friends; then, the next day, enjoyed an exciting tour of the studio. It was most interesting to see the colonial house that was used in "Gone With the Wind," but disappointing to learn that most movie sets were wood and plaster, fake fronts. We had lunch at the

Commissary where we saw a number of well-known stars.

Television was quite new at that time, and I was delighted to be invited to be a guest on an interview show on NBC. Lenore Conn, another girl whom I had met through ham radio, was the star of the show. "What shall I do?" I asked her before the show started.

"Oh," she said, "just be yourself. I'll ask questions about your lighthouse and your radio experiences."

"Should I say the Welland Canal and our lighthouse might one day become an important part of the St. Lawrence Seaway?" I asked.

"Good heavens, no!" Lenore said. "Don't you know that's a controversial subject in this country?"

The interview went very well and Lenore said I acted like a pro. Incidentally, I didn't mention the St. Lawrence Seaway!

This was my first encounter with the opposition that many Americans felt towards the project that we in Canada desired so much. It was quite evident this was a hot issue in the American government at that time.

After the show Maxine said she would like to take us for lunch to the Brown Derby Restaurant nearby. "Leave your studio makeup on, Ethel," she said. "The tourists will think you're a movie star."

I must admit I felt a bit squeamish walking in but I needn't have worried. Not a single person noticed!

Cy and the boys had become quite enthused over television. They shopped around and found a small inexpensive set in a radio store. We pooled our money and bought it.

Our two weeks stay in Los Angeles was over before we realized it. We had enjoyed every minute of our visit and the weather had been ideal. Now we had one week left for our return trip to Canada.

Arriving at the trailer park, en route home, we found our trailer just as we had left it. We slept in it overnight and after fastening it to the car hitch, proceeded to pull it home the next morning. It rode beautifully through heavy snow all the way.

"I guess we gave up too easily," said Cy, a bit sadly. "Enough rubber must have scraped off the tires to give them clearance," he said. "I bet we would have made it to California and back."

"We were lucky Ivan and Margot had enough beds for us," I said. "Our money wouldn't have gone far if we'd had to stay in a motel."

One of the first things Cy did after we arrived home was build a TV antenna on the roof, aimed at Buffalo, New York. This was our nearest television station, and it was a wonderful diversion on those long, chilly nights. We would all sit on the chesterfield, wrapped in blankets and huddled together for warmth, our eyes glued on that nine-inch screen which brought a whole new world into our living room. Sometimes when the wind howled outside and the windows rattled, even Tippy would snuggle under our covers!

When the spring days arrived and a few straggling fishermen wandered down to the lighthouse, the news leaked out; — — the Port Weller Lighthouse has a television set! Many people we barely knew found excuses to visit our lighthouse. Some, who had formerly been casual acquaintances, found their way down the pier. On special nights, when boxing or wrestling matches were featured on TV, every seat in the house was occupied and as many as two rows of youths sitting on the floor.

Television marked the end of our tranquil life at the lighthouse. Never again would we have that wonderful world of our own!

Family in California.

Chapter Fourteen
FRESH WATER -- AT LAST!

Cy had made a little flower garden in front of the house. After digging out clumps of clay and rock, he built a short wall of stones, then filled in the area with topsoil from town. In this we planted a border of dwarf marigolds and a dozen red geraniums. He then put a fence of fine wire net around to keep out the rabbits.

One bright spring morning, when I was cultivating our little garden, I heard a rumbling on the road; I straightened up and saw a big truck approaching.

"Good morning," said the driver, jumping down from his seat. "We've had orders to dig a deep well here."

I could have jumped for joy. How we had longed for this day. No longer would we have to bring fresh water from town.

"Am I ever glad to see you," I said. "My husband is sleeping; would you like me to waken him?"

"Oh, that won't be necessary. We'll scout around to find a likely place to drill. It doesn't look very promising," he added, pointing out the piles of rocks here and there.

I decided they didn't need me, I went indoors to do some housework. Every once in a while I'd look out the window, and each time I saw them digging in a different spot. About two hours later, I screamed out, "Oh, no!" They were digging in the middle of the only soft-looking area on the pier – my flower bed!

I ran outside, rushing like the wind, and managed to rescue some of my precious geraniums. I wouldn't have cared so much if they had found water, but, after drilling down three feet, they stopped working.

"It's useless, Ma'am," one man said. "We'll never get through this rock." Then he said, "Y'know, we have to go down sixty feet to get water. Any less than that we'd only get canal water."

"That's right," I agreed. "I know some people at the beach who had a well drilled and they can't use the water, but please don't give up," I begged him.

"I'm sorry, Ma'am; we've wasted enough time already. Come on, men," he said. "Let's go."

I was desperate; I ran into the house, screaming for Cy. "Oh, Cy," I cried. "The well-diggers are leaving! They say they can't find water."

Aroused from a sound sleep, Cy sat up in bed, in alarm. "What's the matter?" he asked. "Surely they won't go without trying?"

"They dug up my flower bed, but they say it's impossible to dig deep enough. Oh, dear, if they leave now, we won't get them back again!"

Cy pulled his trousers on in a hurry, and I was urging him to come quickly, for I feared they would leave before he had a chance to talk to them.

He strode over to the men, who had already climbed into the truck. "What's going on?" he asked. "I thought you'd come to dig a well."

"I'm sorry, Mr. Williamson, but it can't be done," said the boss. "Why, this pier is nothing but big rocks. Solid rock we can handle, but this stuff is crazy. The rocks are piled up at every angle. We must drill a straight hole before we can put in the casing for the well. With these rocks, the drill slides off; it won't run true."

"Did you try the middle of the pier?"

" No, we didn't. We just thought the whole strip would be the same all the way." He shook his head, and began to walk towards his truck. "It's too bad. We sure would have liked to give you folks fresh water." Then he added, "What makes you think it would be better in the middle of the pier? Isn't it all just a jumble of rocks?"

"Well," said Cy, "I've studied the construction plans of these piers. The banks are made of rock piles, but dirt fill was used down the middle. There may be some rock mixed in, but I'm sure you can drill through." The men looked rather dubious. They were determined to leave. Cy looked desperately from one to the other, then said, "If I can dig down four feet with a shovel, will you give it another try?" They all grinned smugly, but finally agreed to wait and see.

Cy picked up one of the shovels and strode off into the woods. The men followed for about fifty feet, then slumped nonchalantly to the ground, fully convinced that he would quit after a few futile efforts. I stood in the background, watching and praying. If we didn't get our well now, it would be useless to try again.

Cy began to dig. One shovelful, then another and another. It wasn't a hot day, but the sweat streamed down his face. He was now down to clay, and the heavy clods were piling up, as he worked like a maniac. The hole grew deeper and deeper.

One by one, the men got up and took turns at the digging. They hadn't hit rock, yet. At last the boss of the gang admitted the possibility of getting through. He ordered his men to bring the drilling equipment over, and in no time they were at work. About a week later, we had our well; pure, heavenly-sweet well water. An electric pump was installed in the house, and it was simply wonderful to have an unlimited flow of fresh water. No more jars to carry back and forth to the city, and no more sand in our lettuce!

Chapter Fifteen
OUR CAR RUNS INTO THE CANAL!

I really looked forward to my weekly trips into town. I would go to the bank; pay our bills; have a quick look through the shops; a quicker visit with both our mothers; then go to the supermarket for our week's supply of groceries.

No matter how early I started out, it seemed I was always on the last minute coming home for lunch. Cy liked his meals on time, and so I was always in a hurry to get into the house, put on the tea kettle, and set the table. Usually Cy carried in the bags of groceries while I started making our lunch.

One shopping day, when I drove up, in a hurry, as always, Cy was busy repairing something in the Watchroom. I swung the car into the driveway; pulled on the emergency brake; and ran into the kitchen with a couple of parcels. I put the kettle on the burner; then ran out to get a bag of groceries. I set the table; and brought in another bag. The third time out, I made sure the car windows were closed; then proceeded to make lunch.

It must have been half an hour later, while we were eating our dessert, that I heard a car speeding up our road; then there was a screeching of brakes. I ran to look out the kitchen window, and saw a young couple throw open their car doors and jump out.

"Your car's in the canal!" cried the girl, excitedly. "We saw it roll right into the water!"

Cy and I dashed outside, unable to believe our ears. Sure enough, the car was gone! We ran to the canal bank, and there, almost submerged by water, was our car! It seemed impossible, for we hadn't heard a sound!

"It was right there a short while ago," I said. "What could have happened?"

"Are you sure you put the emergency brake on tight?" Cy asked me.

"I'm sure I did," I answered, with a sickening feeling in my stomach. "Oh, dear," I thought, "I hope I did."

"How did you know the car was in the canal?" Cy asked the young man.

"We were having a picnic on the other pier, across from the lighthouse," he said, "when we thought we saw your car slowly creeping backwards towards the canal."

"We were afraid there might be young children inside," said the girl." "and that maybe they had released the brake. It was moving so slowly, we could hardly believe it was happening."

"When it slid down the bank into the water," said the young man, "we couldn't wait any longer. We jumped into our car; drove up the road, and over the bridge; then came down here as fast as we could travel."

"Oh, I do hope there is no one inside," the girl said, fearfully.

"No, thank God," said Cy.

I was very agitated and upset. "I — I'm sure I had the brake on," I insisted.

"There's quite a down grade here," Cy said. "The brake could have slipped." At least he was giving me the benefit of the doubt. The young couple, obviously relieved, returned to their car.

"Will you please have a tow truck sent down?" Cy called, as they turned their car around to drive away.

An hour later, after the car had been hauled to safety, it was a relief to see that the damage was slight. Having water in the engine was the greatest fault. The brake was on, but not as tightly as it should have been. Since then I have never forgotten to put the car in first gear, as a precautionary measure.

Chapter Sixteen
THE PIER'S ON FIRE!

The heavily-wooded piers were a perfect haven for birds and wildlife of many species. Seagulls and crows were with us all year round; and skunks, rabbits and pheasants were plentiful. The spring and fall were special occasions for the invasion of thousands of ducks. At times the canal seemed peppered with ducks. How we loved to watch their antics. Bruce and I spent many happy times trying to guess where they would surface after a deep dive into the water.

I'll never forget one morning in the early spring. It was daybreak. Suddenly I was startled by the sound of what I believed to be a ton of tiny pebbles falling on the roof. I threw my coat on over my nightgown and ran outside to investigate. There, to my surprise, were hundreds of small birds; a variety I had never seen before. They were resting after a long flight from the south.

Later that spring, I noticed a large bird swimming in the canal. It was the largest water fowl I had ever seen. Its long graceful neck moved forward with a slow rhythmic sweep as it propelled itself in the water. "Cy, Cy!" I called. "Come quickly. There's a beautiful bird in the canal. I think it's a black swan."

Cy joined me, and we stepped quietly to the canal bank to get a closer look, and Cy agreed that it was lovely, indeed. "I don't know what it is," he admitted. "I'd like to get a picture."

"Get your camera," I said, "and I'll try to coax him out of the water."

"Optimist!" Cy said, teasingly, as he turned to go into the house.

Softly, I tiptoed to the top of the steps, leading down to the water. The bird was near the dock, seemingly unafraid. While Cy fixed his camera, I went into the house and brought out a crust of bread. I whistled, softly, and held the crust at arm's length. The bird came close I broke off bits of bread and threw some on the rocks, at the water's edge. The bird swam over at once and began eating. I scattered crumbs all the way up the bank, and, lo and behold! it left the water and climbed all the way to the top, eating all the way. I held out the last piece towards him, and he walked right up and ate out of my hand! Cy took this picture.

Some canal watchers happened to be nearby, and they began taking photos of this unusual sight, then, one of them said, "This is the closest I've ever been to a Canada Goose!" Now we knew what the bird was.

Soon after that he flew away, but, to our amazement, he showed up the next day, at about the same time. Again I fed him crusts of bread, and by this time he was following me down the road for more.

"Bread isn't good for him," said Cy. "We'll have to get some grain." I went to the feed store and bought the grain, but Mr. Goose just turned up his nose at that. It was bread he wanted.

Four days later, the local paper sent a reporter down to get a story and some pictures. "Where is your goose?" he asked.

"Oh, he's swimming in the canal," I told him. "Can't you take a picture from here?"

"No," he answered. "I've got orders to take him on the bank, with you feeding him. A human interest story, they want."

"Oh, dear. I don't know when he'll come," I said, "but I'll try calling him." I held a big crust of bread in my hand, and began calling, "Goosey, Goosey, Goosey!" Believe it or not, that big bird swam right over to the canal bank, climbed up the rocks, and took the bread from my hand! The photo was taken, and the next night it was featured at the top of Page Nine of the local newspaper.

There were hundreds of pheasant families in the woods, and a few robins; an occasional racoon, mink or beaver showed up near the water, many mourning doves, red-headed woodpeckers, and wild canaries, and very rarely, a snowy owl.

One day Cy brought a beautiful snowy owl to show me. It had been dead but a short while, for it was still pliable. There was no evidence of the cause of death, but it could have flown into the high light tower, and killed itself. This is one of the tragic kind of accidents that often happen to birds in flight. Thousands are killed at lighthouses every year.

This bird had a wingspread wider than Cy could reach with both arms. It was perfect. "Oh," I cried, "we can't bury him. I'm going to find someone who will mount him, then others will have a chance to admire his beauty." Later, I learned of an engineer on one of the lake ships who did this sort of thing during his winter holidays. He left his ship at Port Weller, Lock 1, long enough to pick up the bird. He wanted to pay us, for he said it was a wonderful specimen, but we refused.

"What will you do with him until the winter?" I asked.

"Oh, I keep my birds in a big freezer until I'm ready to work on them," he said, and off he went with his prize.

Cy reported the incident to the Dept. of Ornithology at the Royal Ontario Museum. This information is useful in special studies that are made in reference to the mass mortality of nocturnal migrants in Ontario. It seems incredible, but the record shows that 5,785 birds of 89 species were killed at lighthouses, towers and tall buildings in three years, in Ontario alone.

Living in the midst of a woods, it was no wonder that one of our worst fears was that of fire. Although fires are prohibited on the piers, many youthful hikers would make a campfire to cook their corn or wieners. We tried to stop them, but it was impossible to see every youngster who wandered through the woods. In fact, some of them were wise enough to slip by on the rocks at the edge of the lake.

Ethel feeds Canada Goose.

Cy was polishing the reflector of the main light one day when he saw curls of smoke above the tree tops, near the end of our west pier. It hadn't rained for weeks, and the grass and trees were parched dry.

Scurrying down the tower steps, he began calling. "Ethel, Ethel, call the office; the pier's on fire!" He ran to the shed, yelling, "Tell them to call the fire department. We must stop it before it reaches the house! I'm going to try to beat it out with brooms."

I thrust two corn brooms into his hands and, holding as many others as he could, he dashed up the road towards the blazing fire, which had now begun to spread. "I'll help, as soon as I get the message through!" I called after him. I ran inside, spun the handle of the battery phone, connecting us to the main office.

After several rings, a voice answered, and I screamed, "The pier's on fire! Phone the volunteer firemen! Hurry, hurry, it's coming towards the lighthouse!" With that, I found two more brooms and ran to help Cy.

Following his example, I began beating the ever-creeping blaze, which gained momentum by the minute, fanned by a brisk north wind. The fire, spreading the entire width of the pier, had swept more than halfway down to the lighthouse. We didn't say a word. If we had, it couldn't have been heard over the deafening roar of the fire. The evergreens, close to the ground, were burning like fireworks; a quick "swoosh," and the tree was enveloped in flames, then loud pops, and shooting sparks, like a giant display. It sounded just like a battlefield, The larger trees burned around the trunks. The only thing Cy and I could do, was to beat out the grass fires.

We dashed wildly from the canal side to the lake side of the pier, beating at the fast-galloping blazes. "Oh," I cried, "where are the firemen? Why don't they come?" I was more angry than afraid. Our brooms were all burnt off to the handles, and we stood there, utterly exhausted, watching the flames speed towards the house.

The fire was less than fifty feet from the buildings, and Cy and I had begun to pack our car with precious belongings, ready for flight, when the firemen arrived. They quickly sprayed the blazing grass and trees with foam fire extinguishers. This worked like a charm. In half an hour there was nothing left but smouldering patches here and there. We stood, numb with fascination, watching the experts at work.

"What, in Heaven's name, took you so long?" Cy asked, later.

"It wasn't our fault," one of the men said. "The guy who called us, just said, 'There's a fire at the lighthouse!' We thought it was Port Dalhousie. We went there first, then we saw your fire from across the lake."

For the first time since the start of the fire, Cy and I really had a chance to look at each other. We both burst out laughing. What a sight we were; black as soot from head to heels. Happy tears of relief ran down our faces 'til we looked like circus clowns. Cy held me in a bear hug, right there, in front of the men. "Spice on the programme," he told the men, with a twinkle in his eyes. We walked hand in hand towards the lighthouse.

"Oh," I cried, bursting out in fresh tears, "think of those lovely birds, and the poor little creatures!"

I'll never forget that moment of despair. The big trees recovered, but the thousands of fir trees were gone forever! Cy tried to comfort me, but it was a long time before I could console myself. How can a person destroy so much by his own carelessness? I determined to be more vigilant than ever. No one would get by me to light a campfire, if I could help it.

Chapter Seventeen

TO THE RESCUE!

One Saturday afternoon Doug and Bruce had driven to town to see a movie. An hour or so later a violent storm blew in. Gale-swept waves lashed over the piers. Through the noisy turmoil of the storm we could hear a plane circling overhead. "He'll never see the light tower!" yelled Cy. We ran outside, but it was impossible to sight the plane, although we could hear it right above our heads. We waited for the crash. Nothing happened. He buzzed over us again. I screamed a warning, forgetting that my voice would be lost in the din all about us.

The plane continued to circle above us while we stood helplessly searching the sky, unable to help in any way. The rain beat our faces, but we couldn't go into the house, knowing that disaster might strike at any moment.

"He must be lost," I cried. "Isn't there some way we can warn him of the tower?"

"We can pray, dear. That's all we can do."

Suddenly the sound was directly above us, and through the fog, we could see a tiny, silver-like plane. We screamed and waved our arms, directing him towards the canal. He swooped down, barely missing us, then he must have seen the water, for without hesitation, he continued his downward flight, making a safe landing in the canal, just 100 yards from our little dock.

"Thank God!" I said; then ran towards the steps to the dock.

Cy was just ahead of me. He turned back to yell, "Go inside!" I paid no attention, but kept on going.

"I said go into the house! I mean it!" he shouted. "The dock's as slippery as ice. You can't help. You'll only be in the way!" I looked down, and could see water washing over the boards. The dock was only visible between waves.

The seaplane bobbed up and down on the water. It was a new aluminum aircraft and, from my position on the bank, it looked like a child's plastic toy. By this time Cy was standing on the dock with waves of water dashing over his feet. Glancing up at me, he yelled, "Scram!" in a tone I couldn't defy.

I ran into the house and tried to peer through the storm from my kitchen window. I couldn't see a thing. I took off my wet clothes and replaced them with fresh dry ones, then tried once more to see what was going on. Finally, no longer able to stand the suspense, I donned a raincoat and kerchief and ran to the top of the steps.

Cy was standing with a rope in his hands, hoping to give the men a line to catch, and so secure them to the dock. I could see two men in the plane, both trying desperately to open the plexi-glass dome that encased them. From their frightened expressions and frantic gestures, Cy could see that they were trapped. Dashing up the steps and brushing past me, he found a crowbar, then ran back down. He motioned for them to taxi closer to the dock, to enable him to get a hold on the plane, but each time they did, waves threatened to dash them on the rocks. Cy's own position on the dock was precarious, too, as he made wild attempts to grab the plane.

"Oh, why must I be a woman, at a time like this!" I cried; but I had enough sense to know I would only add to Cy's troubles if I went down the steps.

After many wild throws, he managed to secure his rope to the plane and pulled it close. Although it bobbed up and down like a cork, he finally managed to insert his crowbar under the dome's edge, and, with a mighty heave, he pried it open. Within seconds both men climbed out and jumped to the dock. At first they were almost incoherent with relief. It had been an awful shock, finding themselves locked in their little plane. Now that they were safely on the ground, they fully realized their narrow escape from death.

Strangers to this part of the country, they'd left Toronto airport for Buffalo, New York, a distance of less than a hundred miles. Caught in a sudden storm, they had lost all sense of direction. After flying blindly for over three hours, they were short on fuel.

Now they realized the desperate situation they had been in. If they had attempted to bale out, the jammed dome would have prevented their escape. Some malfunction had caused it to lock.

They appeared to be arguing with Cy, I couldn't stand the suspense, so I called for him to come up and tell me what was going on. He tried to explain, but I interrupted, to say: "I'll put the coffee pot on the stove, dear, and you invite them up to the house. Y'know something? I think one of the men; the one with a beard, is Ernest Hemingway!" Cy grinned, but shook his head.

"No," he said. "That would be the worse thing to do. These men are scared to death. They want to abandon the plane and go into town. I told them there'd be nothing left of the plane if they left it here, banging into the rocks. I don't want the responsibility of looking after it. They're determined to leave, even if it means walking all the way to town.

"I'm trying to convince them it would be best for them to taxi the plane to the small boat dock. There, it would be safe to leave it overnight, and there would be men to help them. If we encourage them to do that, it would be for the best. They have just enough gas to get that far."

"What about the ships in the canal? They could run into the plane in the fog."

"If you ring the canal office, they'll stop the ships until the plane is in safety. I'll insist on my plan. They must do it."

Disappointed over not meeting the men, I rang the canal office, and, when I explained the situation, I was assured the little plane would be well looked after. A message was sent to halt all shipping below Lock 1, for half an hour, and men were dispatched to give assistance.

Meanwhile, Cy was having difficulties persuading the two men on the dock that everything had been done for their safe passage. Reluctantly, they climbed back into the cockpit of the plane, and, leaving the dome open, they taxied slowly up the canal, and disappeared from sight.

When the boys arrived home they were quite upset to learn they had missed all the excitement. They drove back up the road, crossed the bridge, and came down the east pier, to the small boat dock where they found a crowd of people milling about. It didn't take long for news of anything out-of-the ordinary on the canal to spread.

"Where are the men from the plane?" Doug asked one of the bystanders.

"Oh, they went to town in a taxi," he was told.

The boys called at the canal office, and the clerk said, "The fellows from the plane phoned the airport, and they were told the plane would be re-fuelled in the morning. They decided to stay in a hotel, in town, overnight, and take off in the morning, if the weather clears."

The next morning, about ten o'clock, we heard the roar of the seaplane taking off. Running outside, we saw it lift into the air, then, as it flew over the lighthouse, the silver wings dipped in salute. We never saw or heard of those men again.

Calls to help people in distress came in many guises and in the most unusual circumstances.

In the very early spring, even though the canal is open for navigation, there is often floating ice in the water. It sometimes fills the canal below Lock 1, then, with the movement of ships or a change in the wind, it flows out into the lake only to come back a few hours later.

"Ethel," Cy called out one of the days when the canal happened to be clear of ice, "look at that crazy guy! The minute some fellows get behind the wheel of a boat they lose their heads." We stood at the kitchen window, watching a small outboard motor boat, that appeared to be spanking new. It went forward at top speed; made sharp turns, figure eights, and every kind of tricky maneuver. The two men in the boat seemed bent on testing it to the fullest extent. "The trouble is," said Cy, "if something goes wrong, someone else must risk his life to save them!"

"Brrr," went Doug, who had joined us to watch the men. "I'd hate to have to go into the canal today." The men in the little boat were really taking an awful chance.

After a short while the boat went out into the lake, and we went about our business.

We had forgotten all about the incident until about an hour later, when we were startled to hear a loud banging on the door. I opened it to find a wreched-looking man, shoeless, and soaking wet. He tried to talk, through chattering teeth. I couldn't understand him. "Come inside. Do come in," I begged, "quickly, before you get pneumonia." Needing no urging, he almost collapsed into my arms. Cy and Doug helped him into a chair.

"Now," said Cy, "tell us what happened."

"My boat capsized!" the man gasped. "It's on the rocks — smashing on the rocks. My friend — he's hurt. He's trying to hold onto the boat. I came for help."

I wrapped a heavy blanket around him, and soon his shivering lessened. "I was trying out my new boat," he told us.

"We saw you in the canal," Cy spoke roughly. "You were doing all kinds of crazy stunts. Guys like you should never have a boat," he added, with disgust. "What about your pal? If he's hanging onto the boat he's in real trouble."

The man looked down, shamefacedly, then admitted, "Neither of us can really swim. We managed to right the boat, and pulled it to the pier. I tied the rope around a big rock but it won't stay there very long, with those big waves. My friend, Bill — he's hurt his leg. He's lying on the bank, holding onto another rope."

"Just whereabouts is he?" asked Cy, as he donned a heavy jacket, preparing to go out to find the fellow.

"The boat capsized just as we attempted to go around the west pier. I'd say he's on the lakeside of the pier, about 100 yards from the end."

"I'm coming with you, Dad," called Doug, as Cy went out the door. I handed a couple of blankets to Doug as he dashed after his father. I felt disgusted too. Why should my men have to risk their lives trying to save such foolish fellows? Just the same I knew they must help anyone in distress. My job was to care for this poor creature, even though I was raging with anger inside.

"You'd better get out of those wet clothes," I told him. "I'll run some warm water in the tub, and find you a pair of pyjamas. D'you think you can get into the tub?" I asked, rather reluctantly. All at once I had a scary feeling that I might have to put my Red Cross training to the test. What a relief when he assured me he was quite capable of climbing into the tub!

He was in the bathroom so long I was just beginning to fear the worst, when he finally emerged in the pyjamas and an old bathrobe, looking more like a human being. I poured out a cup of hot coffee. He relaxed as the comforting liquid went down; the colour came back into his cheeks, and we sat at the kitchen table, trying to make small talk, and trying not to worry too much about the others.

It seemed to be such a long wait, actually more than an hour, before the car returned. Cy and Doug helped the other man out of the car, and half carried him into the kitchen. He was in a sorry state; wet to the skin; shaking as if he had palsy, and limping rather badly.

"Doug!" I cried, "you're all wet too!" He shook his head and made a futile gesture with his hands.

"I had to dive in to grab the rope," he explained.

"Why did you have to do that?"

"Well, we thought we could make the boat secure by tying as many ropes to it as possible."

"It was a good job we took more ropes," said Cy. "We were able to put three lines on it. It should keep it there until morning; unless a storm blows in. It's really none of my business but I hate to see a lovely new boat ruined through carelessness. Doug and I managed to save the engine. We unfastened it and carried it up the bank. I think it'll be all right."

By this time Doug and the other chap were undressed, and wrapped in warm blankets. Cy had helped the injured man disrobe, and after he had rested for a few minutes, he helped him into the bathtub. It wasn't too long before they all felt warm and comfortable. The injured ankle of the second man was wrapped in a bandage, and he was resting it on a big cushion.

"I think it's only a sprain," Cy told me, "but he mustn't put any pressure on it until he's seen a doctor." Cy had brushed aside my attentions, saying he could look after himself, but I was worried about him. His cheeks, normally rosy pink, were pale and drawn. It was quite evident that he had been over-straining himself as he often did in times of stress. I couldn't help thinking of how much is expected of a big man.

"Our wives are waiting for us at Lock 1," said one of the men. "They have our boat trailer hooked to the station wagon."

I could well imagine them in a desperate state of anxiety. They must have guessed by this time that something was wrong. Cy offered to drive to the lock, find the women and tell them of the accident. We all waited their arrival with concern, for it must have been an awful shock to learn about the accident.

At last they came down the road, following Cy. I held the door open wide, for I knew they would be anxious to see for themselves that their husbands were safe and sound. A Big-Bertha-type woman pushed me aside; strode into the centre of my kitchen, and, literally blazing with anger, faced her husband.

"Where's the boat?" she demanded. "I said, where's the boat? What happened to it?"

The poor man made a feeble effort to explain, but she continued to storm on about the boat. Not one word of concern about the condition of her husband! I felt sick to my stomach.

I was never so happy to see anyone leave. They told us they would be back early the next morning with a crane, to haul the boat up the canal bank. "We'll drop these clothes off when we come by," they promised. I rolled up their wêt things and handed them to Big Bertha. I wanted nothing more to do with them.

The next day, a gang of men hoisted the boat onto a trailer and the next thing we knew they were speeding past the house. We never heard from them again; not even to return the borrowed clothing.

Chapter Eighteen

THE YEARS SLIP BY

The years slipped by like ships on the canal. Bruce, now eighteen, and never serious about schoolwork, had finished his last year at Collegiate.

Cy, quite upset because Bruce had no plans for the future, questioned him. "What do you want to be?" he asked. "What do you expect to do with your life?"

Bruce looked crestfallen for a moment, then, his face lighting up with a mischievous grin, he announced, "A Playboy! That's what I'd like to be!"

"A Playboy!" Cy shouted. He didn't think it funny at all. "I warned you, young man, if you don't know what you want to do I'll find you a job where you'll learn a trade, and by George, I will! You're going to learn the value of money and honest work," he said. "Tomorrow, I'm taking you to see the Publisher of The Standard" (our local newspaper).

"Oh, Dad, my friends'll laugh at me. Why, the other guys I know are going to work in factories, – and they're getting high wages, too."

"You'll be able to laugh at them a few years from now," said Cy. "You'll have a trade – a good trade – and they'll still be labourers."

The next day, Bruce, light-heartedly, as usual, went with Cy to see Henry Burgoyne, owner and Publisher of The St. Catharines Standard. After a brief interview, Bruce was accepted as a Printer's Devil. Strangely enough, he loved the work from his very first day. "It's just like being part of a happy family," he told us.

Douglas, now an accountant at the bank, had become engaged to Effie Gifford, a tall, slim girl with curly, chestnut brown hair, twinkling greenish eyes and lovely warm smile. They had worked at the same bank for over a year. Cy and I were delighted. He could have searched the world over and not found a nicer girl or one more suitable for him. They had a lovely wedding, and the next year presented us with our first grandson, Douglas Jr.

Another blessing that year was the installation of a telephone. After all these years, the telephone company had finally reached my application! It took three miles of line and many poles to bring the phone to the lighthouse, and we shared the line with nineteen others, at Port Weller Beach, but it was a godsend!

Then came more good news. The Department of Transport was going to build us a new home. It would be about thirty feet south of our present dwelling, which would then accommodate an assistant lightkeeper. This meant that Cy would have full-time helper.

We had many interesting visitors that summer. What joy to greet people from India, France, Denmark, Mexico, England and The Netherlands! Ham radio had introduced us to these fascinating friends from other lands but it was the lighthouse and its aura of romance that had brought them to our home. One lady from England sat for hours on the canal bank, just watching the ships sail by. "It's simply smashing!" she exclaimed.

One day two ladies from Malta called on us. I decided to show off a little on my radio. I really took quite a risk, for ham radio, like small children, can prove temperamental and unresponsive just when one expects a smooth performance. I took the microphone, and called, "CQ, CQ, CQ, VE3DTW in Canada is calling CQ."

Immediately came a reply. "Hello, VE3DTW. This is PZ1J, Paramaribo, Surinam, Netherlands Guiana. I hope you remember me Ethel; this is Julian Archer."

I did remember him, very well, for we had enjoyed many chats over the air. I introduced my guests, and after an animated and delightful exchange between people of three nationalities, we signed off; everyone agreeing that this must surely be an instrument of peace, whereby men could communicate, and learn that we aren't so much different after all.

Next to Niagara Falls, the Welland Canal has been the second most popular tourist attraction in the Niagara District. Many of the thousands of visitors spend hours following a ship's progress through all the eight locks, from one lake to the other. This procedure takes about eight hours, and at each lock the tourists can get close enough to the ship to chat with members of the crew.

Maxine Willis, W6UHA of Los Angeles, California and Ethel, VE3DTW.

My greatest joy that summer was the first visit of my friend, Maxine. What a pleasure it was to have a guest who was so delighted with everything she saw, from the country to the people. From that time until today, Maxine has called Canada her second home. During her ten-day stay, I was able to drive her all over the Niagara Peninsula. During the Lakeshore drive to Niagara-on-the-Lake, Queenston and Niagara Falls, I said, "This is the same route taken by the King and Queen in 1939."

She smiled, and said, "I'm sure they have never seen anything more beautiful in all their travels. I know I haven't."

Maxine is known all over the world as one of the most popular girl hams, having contacted the highest number of foreign countries. While at our lighthouse, she was interviewed and photographed by newsmen and, just before she left, we had a big party, inviting all hams in the district to meet her.

Chapter Nineteen
ILLNESS STRIKES

Another summer had slipped by. Work on our new house was progressing nicely, and we were eagerly looking forward to moving in. It was World Series time, and Bruce, an avid sports fan, was on holidays, and had decided to go to New York for a week to watch the games. Doug had spoken so glowingly of his visit to New York that Bruce was really keen to go. This would be his first time away from home. How we would miss his cheery remarks and silly antics!

Soon after Bruce left, Cy was taken ill!

I was awakened in the middle of the night by terrifying loud groans! Running into the Watchroom, I found Cy doubled over with pain.

"What is it, dear?" I cried in alarm. "What happened?"

Cy's face was contorted with agony. He couldn't answer for a few minutes, then he spoke, chokingly.

"I — I don't know. It happened so quickly. I, I've got a terrible pain in my chest. — I can't straighten up. — My left arm seems dead. — I can't get my breath!"

It had taken several minutes for him to tell me all this. I just stood there, numb with fear and anxiety. I'd never seen Cy like this before. Cy, such a tower of strength! How could anything like this happen to him? I felt utterly lost and helpless.

Finally, I asked, "What can I do, dear? I must call a doctor."

"Maybe it's just indigestion," Cy muttered. "Get me some baking soda." His face was contorted with pain.

I quickly brought a glass of water with some baking soda, and he tried to sip a little of it. "I hate to ask a doctor to drive all the way out here at this time of morning," he said.

A hundred wild thoughts raced through my mind. A doctor? Who could I get? Our family doctor had died recently. We were a remarkably healthy family, and hadn't needed the services of a doctor in several years. Who would come to a stranger at three o'clock in the morning, and seven miles from town?

"Try to relax, dear," I said. "You should be in bed."

"I — I can't lie down. I've tried. It only makes the pain worse."

"How about the heating pad? Would that help?"

"It might. I'll try anything." Beads of perspiration ran down his face. I helped him into a comfortable chair, then went to get the electric pad.

"Let me call a doctor, dear," I pleaded, wringing my hands in despair. The pad was warm now, and Cy held it to his chest.

"It's awful to feel so helpless," I said. "I can't bear to see you in so much pain."

"I feel easier since you gave me this heat," he said, then added, "I'll try to hold on till morning. You can call someone about eight o'clock. Guess I'll have to sit here; can't move. Will you keep watch for me, honey?"

"You know I will, dear. I'll call a doctor as soon as you let me. I'll have to phone Prescott, too. They must send someone to take over your duties until you get well."

I tried to make Cy comfortable with pillows and a blanket, then, feeling chilly, I made a pot of tea. I dressed in warm clothes, and prepared to take over the night watch. We passed those early morning hours in fear and trepidation. It was an eternity.

At daylight, I called a doctor of internal medicine. After a thorough examination, and an electrocardiagraph, he told us Cy had probably had a heart attack, but it seemed the worst was over. The main treatment was complete rest. He should be in hospital.

I telephoned the head office in Prescott to tell them of Cy's condition, and asked them to send a replacement for a few weeks. They expressed concern; but this had happened at a time when it was impossible to send a man capable of taking charge. When I told Cy, he said he would tell the doctor of the circumstances; and ask if he could possibly stay at home. I knew enough about the station to keep watch, check the radio beacon for correct timing, and operate all switches for lights, foghorn, and so on. If no replacement was available, I would have to take over, providing Cy was there to guide me in case of an emergency.

The doctor told us of the dangers involved, but said Cy would be all right as long as I could keep him perfectly quiet, in bed. This we had to do; there was no other choice. How thankful I felt for my training in radio; otherwise, I would have been helpless.

"Be sure to call us if Cy has another attack," the marine agent told me, "or if an emergency arises which you can't handle. Good luck," he said.

I hung up the receiver; closed my eyes tightly, and prayed, "Please God, don't let the main light go out. I just can't climb that awful tower!"

The thought of going up those steel steps at night, alone, was terrifying, and yet, I knew it might have to be done.

Doug and Effie came as soon as they heard of Cy's attack. They wanted to help in any way they could, but Doug had his work and Effie had the baby.

The agent called to ask how things were. I assured him everything would be fine. "Bruce will be home in a couple of days," I said. "He'll take over." Cy had taught both boys many of the routine tasks of lightkeeping. This was a blessing now.

The weather remained clear. The radio beacon and motors ran smoothly. My chief problem was lack of sleep. I had to keep watch all night, and try to nap in the daytime, after attending to my patient. This proved to be almost impossible, due to the construction noises on the new house, just a few feet away. I was desperately tired.

On the fifth day after Cy's attack Bruce arrived home. I'd never been more eager to greet him. No matter what happened now, I wouldn't have to climb that formidable light tower!

After two weeks Cy had x-rays at the hospital. This doctor said he thought Cy had a hiatus hernia. Then a specialist was consulted. He disagreed, and suggested an exploratory operation to find the trouble.

Cy was so confused and upset, he had no faith in either man. He decided to wait and see. And so, armed with nitro-glycerine tablets for emergencies, and pain killers, he determined to carry on; avoiding strenuous activities, and eating a light diet. He felt much better in a few weeks, but from then on there would always be this nagging worry in our minds. The attack, if it really was the heart, had been slight. What wonderful relief to know he would soon have a full-time assistant to help him with the lighthouse duties!

By mid-November, 1953, our new house was finished. What a delight it was choosing my favourite colours for walls and rugs! We bought more pieces of Canadian maple furniture and my collection of milk glass looked beautiful on the shelves of the corner cupboard.

The modern cottage had full insulation and an automatic oil furnace. All windows allowed a clear view of the lake or the canal. From my kitchen window, facing north, I watched the ships entering the canal harbour. I could never count the times I left dishes in the sink and grabbed the binoculars, to get a better view. Sunrise, sunset, ships and birds; what more could anyone desire? There was always something to see; strange ships from foreign countries; now and then a beautiful passenger ship, taking hundreds of people on a holiday cruise; a fancy yacht or sailboat, or young people water-skiing.

From the south window of the living room I saw a different view. Here were all the activities below Lock 1. I could see the ships tied up below the lock, and others which seemed to tower over these, as the water level in the lock raised them to the same height as the canal above. It was just lovely!

Cy built a garage and a breezeway between the two houses which made a fine windbreak, for, as the Watchroom was still in the old house, he had to travel back and forth many times a day. He also installed a radio monitor in our kitchen, so he could listen in on the radio beacon, and be alerted if he heard any unusual sound coming from the Watchroom.

Chapter Twenty

WE VISIT RADIO FRIENDS ABROAD

For months, our radio friends, overseas had urged us to visit them on our winter holidays. "Do come," they begged. "We'll give you a wonderful time." Well, the outcome of all their warm invitations was that we decided to go. Cy had often told me he would take me to see some of the places he had known during the war, but until now we'd never dreamed that this would become a reality.

The lighthouse had made our dreams come true. Having three months' holiday allowed us enough time for a leisurely stay, and the kind hospitality offered by our radio friends was too tempting to refuse. How could we resist?

The excitement grew. As soon as our plans were known, invitations poured in by the dozen. It would have taken a year's holiday to accept them all!

One day, while chatting to a friend in Addis Ababa, Ethiopia, I mentioned our proposed trip to Europe. He laughingly remarked, "I'll be in London in March. Wouldn't it be fine if we should meet?"

"Who knows?" I answered. "Miracles do happen." We both had a good laugh at the absurdity of the idea. How impossible this would be in that city of millions!

As the winter closing of navigation drew nearer, we rushed ahead with our plans. Our departure was set for the 30th of December, on the Queen Elizabeth, from New York. This meant that we would be able to spend Christmas with our children and parents. Doug and Effie would come to spend the winter in our new house and to be company for Bruce. They looked forward to having lots of fun. We made arrangements to keep in touch with them, by radio, from each place we visited on the weekends.

We took a trunkful of gifts for our friends, and were advised to have it bonded, so that it needn't be opened for customs in New York. Arriving in that city, we spent most of two days locating the trunk, for it had been misplaced by the railway. With only hours to spare, we found it, and made our way to the ship on time.

New Year's Eve aboard the Queen Elizabeth was a gala affair, but I'm sorry to say I turned out to be a poor sailor. Luckily, Cy found a friend – a young Danish chap, who was returning to Denmark after a business trip to the United States. While I forced myself to swallow lemon juice and glucose, and begged Cy to leave me alone in my misery, he and his friend went to the movies, played cards and ate everything on the menu from top to bottom. The moment the ship anchored at Southampton, I recovered.

Everyone assured me it had been a very rough voyage, but just the same I couldn't help feeling a bit shamefaced, and tried to put aside the knowledge that I would have to return the same way.

The train ride to London was quite an experience. We found ourselves seated across a narrow table from two young people, a brother and sister from India. The young man wore western clothing but his sister was dressed in a lovely sari, and had a red dot painted on her forehead. We introduced ourselves; then, when a waiter came for our order, we all asked for tea and cakes.

As we sipped tea, we began an animated conversation. They seemed eager to tell of their experiences. "We have been taking post-graduate courses in New York City," said the youth. "Now we must visit London before going home to India. We're anxious to see the museums and all the historical places."

Just then the train stopped at a little station. I noticed the girl's eyes filled with tears. "The station — " she said, haltingly, "it makes me homesick. It's just like our stations in India."

"Naturally," said her brother. "After all, were not our stations built by the British?"

Soon we were rolling past little country villages. The green clipped hedges, winding roads and tiny houses with their hundreds of chimney pots — each blowing a trail of smoke — greenhouses in every backyard and little gardens of brussels sprouts; suddenly it all hit me. — This is England! My eyes were blinded for a moment by tears, then I noticed the Indian girl . . . She was crying too! "It's really true," she cried. "It is England!" Suddenly, at the same moment, we had realized that everything we had once read about could now be seen. It brought back memories of Charles Dickens' books, and all the beautiful poems I'd read describing the English countryside.

A group of English friends met us at Waterloo Station and drove us to a dear little home in Ewell, a small suburb of London. There, amidst warm-hearted, kindly people and happy talk, we were entertained at our first "tea," an early evening meal which we in Canada might call supper. This was the beginning of a wonderful holiday. What a delight to meet our radio friends in person! Everyone seemed nicer than we had imagined. It was great fun matching the people to their voices; the closest we had known them until now.

Cy took great pleasure in showing me around London. It was a far different place than he had known in wartime, and there were now many places of interest opened to the public that had been closed during the war.

We had made arrangements to talk by radio to our families in Canada, each weekend.

"Don't hurry back," they told us. "We're having a ball!" I had thought it would be lonely for Effie while the fellows were at work, instead, she assured us she was enjoying the peace and quiet of the lighthouse. She took pleasure in making a nice dinner each night, and having spare time for sewing and reading. Doug told us: "Believe it or not, Bruce and I have really got to know each other more these weeks than we ever had before. We have never been better friends."

I couldn't help recalling a bitter fight they had when Cy was overseas. I managed to separate them.

Later, I heard Bruce whisper to Doug, "Just wait till I'm as big as you: we'll have a fight to the death!"

Now they were grown men, and it was heart-warming to know they were so close.

A letter came from my friend, Louise ten Herkel, in The Hague. "Do come to Holland soon," she pleaded. "Remember, we have central heating." This was an added enticement, for she had heard all about the little fireplaces in the English homes. Cy and I had been so overwhelmed by the warm hospitality we found on every hand, we had little time to worry about minor inconveniences. We had, however, planned a trip to the Continent, and soon we were sailing across the English Channel to Holland.

Louise and Hans, her husband, met us at the railway station. We embraced like old friends. They lived in an attractive home, that had housed the High Command of the German Occupation Forces during the war. "They just ordered us to vacate," Louise told us. "We didn't get it back until the Canadians arrived to liberate us."

One highlight of this visit was an invitation to speak over PCJ, the famous radio station. My message was to be transmitted all over the world. Louise and I were both in tears when the time came for us to part.

From Holland, we went to Belgium. We stayed at the Atlanta Hotel, Brussels, where many Canadians were housed after the war.

A week in Paris seemed to transport us to another world. Simply walking the streets, soaking in the beautiful architecture of the buildings was pure joy. Everywhere we travelled, we met radio friends, and we were never disappointed when we saw them in person. It was all so unbelievable. Was this really Cy and Ethel in the Hall of Mirrors; at the Louvre; on the Seine? Walking through Sherwood Forest and climbing the steps of the Tower of London to see the Crown Jewels?

We found a warm welcome everywhere, from the tiny cottage of a pensioner to the baronial estate of a Scottish lumber merchant. All these friends we had met through a mutual, world-wide hobby, and the aura of interest envisioned and aroused by our unique occupation. Only through ham radio could we have found so many friends in so many places; from so many walks of life; and our lighthouse gave us enough vacation time to make this wonderful trip possible. Surely this was the perfect way to become a true Cosmopolite; to accept and love people of any nationality under so many diverse conditions.

When our holiday was nearly over, we were guests of honour at a party in the home of a fellow Canadian, near London. Earlier in the evening a phone call came from London.

"Sorry I can't come to your party," the caller said. "An old friend has just arrived from abroad."

"Is he a ham?" asked our host.

"As a matter-of-fact he is."

"Well, then, bring him along; we'd like to meet him."

An hour later, I happened to be near the front door when I heard a knock. I opened the door and found two young men. One had a dark tan and a mop of curly yellow hair. "Do come in," I said. "I'm VE3DTW, Ethel Williamson from Canada."

"And I," said Yellow Mop, a wide grin lighting his face, "am Harry Dell, from Addis Ababa, Ethiopia!"

Meeting our radio friends in person was always a delightful and oft-times surprising occasion, but I think our greatest surprise was our old Scottish friend, Frank, GM8MN.

From his thick brogue and jolly laugh, I had pictured him to be a little old man, wearing a kilt, showing his knobby knees and carrying a crooked cane, like Harry Lauder. He had often talked about being an old sea dog, and, judging from his banter over the air, I assumed him to be an old bachelor, living alone in the hills.

When Frank learned that we would be going to Europe, he insisted on us paying him a visit in Crieff, Scotland. Even though he would be the only ham we would be calling on in Scotland, we felt we must make a special effort to go there. We had grown to love the old codger, just through his voice, and our memorable conversations. We took a train north, from London, prepared for anything.

Frank met us at the station, impeccably dressed, the antithesis to our expectations. We were driven in a handsome, Humber Super Snipe car, to his beautiful home, set amidst formal gardens; met his charming wife, Jessie, and the rest of his family; dined on partridges, in a formal dining room; and were served breakfast in bed the next morning!

When we told him of our mistaken impression of him, he roared with laughter. A lumber merchant, with many business ventures, he had found ham radio a perfect hobby; for here he could relax, and completely forget the pressures of business.

Chapter Twenty-one

SEAWAY PLANS APPROVED

HURRICANE HAZEL CALLS

Great excitement filled the air these days, for, after waiting many years for the Americans to join in the Seaway Project, Canada, who had passed the bill authorizing it in 1951, had decided to build it alone, if necessary.

Many influential Americans had fought against the plan; other powerful forces were in favour. President Eisenhower was finally instrumental in having Congress pass legislation for a joint effort with Canada in the building of the St. Lawrence Seaway and Power Project. Work began on the gigantic project on August 19, 1954, with international sod-turning ceremonies at Cornwall, Ontario and Massena, New York.

Thus began the world's greatest inland navigation system.

Although this news was most exciting, especially to us at the lighthouse, for we knew the Welland Canal would be one of the most important links in this great chain of waterways to be called the St. Lawrence Seaway, it was still in the planning stage, and would take years to complete.

Much more imminent and important to us at the lighthouse was the news of Hurricane Hazel. Radio, television and newspapers had been telling for days of the devastation and loss of life in the wake of this storm. This wicked witch was following no predictable pattern, but striking here and there with little or no warning. The hurricane hit the eastern part of the United States with terrific force, causing millions of dollars damage, and now it seemed to be heading north in a startling and unprecedented pattern. We had come through some frightening storms during the past years, but nothing to equal the violence of this infamous lady.

Blithely we went about our business, feeling sympathy for those who had suffered loss of family or property, but as yet totally unaware of the danger that was heading in our direction.

In the morning of October 16, 1954, Doug, Effie and little Doug came down to see Cy's new boat. It was an outboard cruiserette; a beautiful little craft with twin engines. Bruce had bought water skis, and we all looked forward to trying to ski on the smooth water of the canal.

After lunch, Cy came down from the main light tower. His face was drawn with anxiety. "I'm afraid there won't be any more boating or skiing to-day," he announced. "The lake is rough; a strong wind is stirring everything up. It looks like Hazel's coming our way." By this time Hazel had become a household word. We knew what it meant. Where would it strike? What damage would it do? We would soon know.

Although Cy's concern for his new boat was uppermost in his mind, his lighthouse duties must come first. While he and I dashed about locking and securing everything against the storm, Doug and Bruce took care of the boat. They had to fasten the lower part of the canvas, by standing in the rowboat, and maneuvering around the new boat, with both boats bobbing up and down in the rough water. Every movement strained the ropes that tied her to the dock. It started to rain. The canvas ballooned with each gust of wind. It seemed as if it would blow away any minute.

Back in the house, the television showed parts of Toronto in the throes of distress, where Hazel was raging without letup. Yes, it was only a matter of minutes before we'd feel the full force of the storm. Doug yelled up from the dock, "We want to take her up to the small boat dock, Dad."

"Can you make it? You've only sailed her once." With assurances that they could, Cy added, "Well — OK, but it'll be a rough ride." Then he called, "I don't know, fellows. It isn't worth risking your lives."

This was met with a storm of protest. "Look, Dad; we're grown men; we can take care of ourselves!"

Effie and I were dead against the idea, but once it was agreed upon nothing would stop them. While we watched from the house, the fellows undid as much of the canvas as would allow them to scramble aboard. Cy untied all the restraining ropes but one, holding onto that like grim death, until both engines roared into action. Everything had been planned beforehand, for words were just wasted in the wild roar of the wind.

Luckily, the wind and current were with them, as they shot out into the middle of the canal, heading for Lock 1. In seconds they were out of sight; lost in the fury of the storm. Cy phoned the office to send men over to help them, and was assured that they would be driven back to the lighthouse, as soon as the little craft was securely tied in the small boat dock. Just the same, Effie and I prayed that they would get there safely. Cy was worried too, but he knew they were in a sturdily-built boat, and he was confident that the boys would do their best.

Suddenly, Effie cried out, "Oh, the poor roses; look at them!" The wind was blowing them at right angles. Many of the blooms had already blown into the canal. "I'm going to cut some before they're all gone!" she said, pulling on her jacket. She was just about to run out, when we saw the picnic table fly through the air. It landed in the canal, and was soon carried away with the waves. That stopped her. Then, we heard a terrible crash in another direction. The wooden tower and radio antenna had blown off the roof of the other building. Just as the boys drove up, the power went dead. We hurried them into the house; got them to change into dry clothing, and poured out cups of hot coffee. Throughout all this noise and excitement, we had managed to hide our fears from little Dougie. He thought it was fun!

With the power off, everything went dead. Cy tried to call the power house but our telephone was out too. With the acquisition of a Bell telephone, the canal had disconnected our old battery phone.

"A tree must have fallen across the wires," Cy announced "I'll have to drive to the canal office to report the trouble."

"I'll go with you, Dad," said Bruce.

"OK, Bruce," said Doug, "I'll stay here to look after the girls."

"Be careful, honey," I warned. "I'll have supper ready when you get back."

It would be quite a job cooking supper for six on our old gasoline camp stove by flickering candlelight; but I'd done it many times on camping trips in the old days. We had taken refuge in the basement at the height of the storm, and there we sat, desperately trying to make light of the situation, while Doug kept watch upstairs. Every once in a while he'd call down to tell us the latest.

It seemed like hours before the fellows returned. Cy's hunch had proven correct. A tree had fallen across the lines. Canal workers were already at work making repairs. All aids to navigation were stopped until power was restored. A radio message had been transmitted to all shipping and everyone was on the alert.

"We sure had a rough time going up the road," Cy told us. "Broken branches, dead leaves and heavy rain were bad enough, but Oh, Boy! when we reached the sandpile and the soft coal, it was murder!"

"Maybe we should go over to the old house?" I said. "It's solid concrete; nothing could budge that." We talked it over, but decided to remain in the basement.

Doug had found an old coal-oil lamp in the shed, and now its soft glow helped keep away that scary feeling in the heart of each of us, while all hell was popping outside.

"I wonder what it's like in the city?" asked Effie.

"The fellows in the canal office said it wasn't too bad in town, but Toronto has been taking a beating. We'll hear all about it when the power's back on; that is unless the radio stations are off the air too."

This news disturbed us, but we tried to make jokes to keep up our spirits. Dougie was the only one who was unconcerned; to him this was all a game.

When the power was restored, it was too dark outside to estimate the damage. The next morning, however, it looked like a cyclone had hit the pier.

Everywhere we looked, we saw broken trees, piles of debris and tangled wire. We spent the weekend helping Cy clear up the mess. It wasn't nearly as much fun as boating or water-skiing, but oh, now fortunate we had been! We all agreed we would never forget the day that Hurricane Hazel passed our way!

Chapter Twenty-two
HAPPENINGS

One morning in the early spring we heard a "toot toot" from the boat dock. It was too foggy to see who was calling us, so we ran down the steps and found a small outboard boat beside the dock.

"Could we tie-up here for a while?" A young man called from the boat.

"Sure," said Cy. "You'll be all right as long as it stays calm. Here, throw your line to me; I'll fasten it to the dock."

In a few minutes the little craft "Moonstruck" was securely tied, and we invited the man, Kenneth Wells, and his wife, Lucy to come into the house for a visit.

"Can I make a long distance phone call?" asked Lucy. "I must let our family in Toronto know we're all right."

"I'd like to call Toronto, too," said Ken. "I'll have to tell the reception committee that we're fogbound, and won't be able to cross the lake until the weather clears."

After the calls were made, we chatted as we drank coffee, and they told us a remarkable story.

Ken was a well-known writer, and Lucy did woodcuts to illustrate his books. They both loved sailing, and when they decided to sail their eighteen-foot, single engine, outboard cruiser down the Mississippi River to the Gulf of Mexico, and return by the inland waterways, then write a book about their experiences, a publisher gave them an advance on the book. A motor company agreed to give them the engine, provided they allowed publicity for his product.

They left their home near Toronto in the fall of the previous year; sailed down the Mississippi to New Orleans, then, after a cruise around the West Indies, they returned to the north by way of the inland waterways of Florida to the Atlantic Ocean. Reaching New York City, they sailed up the Hudson River to the Erie Canal; the Erie Canal to Lake Erie, and the southern entrance to the Welland Canal, at Port Colborne.

Sailing through the canal they found the fog thickening more by the minute, and by the time they reached our lighthouse, they knew it would be impossible to cross Lake Ontario to Toronto.

Now I knew what the whole thing was about, I was more intrigued than ever.

"Isn't it awful?" Lucy declared. "Just think; only thirty miles from home, after nearly six months, and sailing more than 6000 miles; and this is our first really bad break!"

"Yes," Ken added, "and imagine how this will upset all the plans of the reception committee. They're going to have a band; TV cameras; the whole works. Wouldn't it be terrible if we should have a mishap so close to home?"

"You're welcome to stay here until the fog clears," Cy told them.

"Thank you," said Ken. "We'd really appreciate that; however, we must stay on the boat. That's our agreement."

By late afternoon, reporters, having learned of the "Moonstruck," docked at the Port Weller Lighthouse, arrived to take photos and write their stories for the newspapers. It was front page news.

Ken and Lucy were with us for three days before the fog lifted, and they could sail away to Toronto.

That evening, on television, Cy and I were delighted to watch the formal reception, tendered by the city of Toronto, and to know we had played a small part in their safe arrival.

We were having a family picnic on the lawn behind our house, one sunny Saturday afternoon, when piercing cries broke the stillness of a perfect summer day. Startled, we all ran to the lakeside of the pier, to find a cabin cruiser heading straight for the rocks.

"Why, the guy's crazy!" yelled Cy. "Something must be wrong."

We could see a young man, a woman and two young girls; and they were yelling and waving their arms like wild people. The man turned off his engine, as the boat ran into the rocks, and he called, "Help us! For God's sake, help us!"

Our men scrambled down the rocky bank, and caught the rope lines as they were thrown from the boat. "Help the girls!" the man cried. "They can't swim, and our boat is sinking!"

Well, it didn't take long to get the woman and girls off the boat, over the rocks, and up the bank of the pier. They were terrified, and it was a few minutes before we could make sense of their stories.

The young man and wife had bought the cruiser just the night before. They had paid cash for it, by cheque; several thousand dollars. It wasn't a new boat, but to one unfamiliar with these things, it seemed in perfect condition. They had set out for their first sail, filled with joy and anticipation, but, just three miles from shore they discovered the hold was filling with water. Desperate, the man headed for our pier, hoping to reach it before his boat sank into the lake.

We looked after the girls while the men tried to secure the boat. It was a large cruiser, and it required a big crane to lift it up the bank. It was half filled with water before the crane arrived, and it was past midnight before the boat was finally hauled out of the water. A dry rot condition had caused the boat to deteriorate so quickly, once it was in the water, and it was a miracle that the little family survived.

Cy's duties became much easier at this time for he now had an assistant keeper. It was his father, a retired painter. He and Mother moved into the original dwelling, and, at long last, a furnace was installed, making it much more comfortable.

Cy's mother and I had always been good friends, and it was so nice to have a neighbour. Painting was a never-ending job at the lighthouse; so Dad was a valuable helper. They both loved gardening, and this too saved Cy hours of time.

One day Mother called, "I just saw a deer jump the fence!" We had seen many wild creatures in the woods but never a deer. I joined her, and ran through the trees, looking for it, but it had disappeared.

Before Christmas, when Cy and I went looking for evergreen branches to decorate the house, we stopped dead in our tracks. There, stretched between branches of a tree was the hide of a deer! Hunters, who must have sneaked past the house, had killed him; taken the meat, and left the skin to dry. We were horrified, and Cy reported it to the canal officials, but nothing could be done.

We now thought of Bruce as our bachelor son. He loved his newspaper work, and was now a journeyman-printer. He and Cy had a fine relationship. I loved to see them having such good times together, playing table-tennis, swimming and water skiing.

He was a real home boy, and although I often teased him about girls, he'd laugh it off.

"Leave him alone," Cy would say. "When the right girl comes along, he'll know it."

Bruce stayed at the lighthouse, with his grandparents that winter while Cy and I went to California again on our holidays. When we returned, Mother whispered, "Bruce has a girlfriend. Don't tell him I've told you; but she's a lovely girl. I know you'll like her."

During supper the next evening, Bruce, smiling shyly, said, "I'd like to bring a girl home tonight, Mother." Then, "I hope you'll approve."

"What's her name?" I asked, hoping to sound convincingly unaware, for Mother had already told me the details.

"Beverley," he said, "Beverley Hillier."

"Why," I said, "I know her parents; don't I?"

"Yes, Mother. They know you and Dad. Is it OK?"

I gave him a big hug. I didn't need to tell him how very pleased this news made me.

Bev was nineteen; a lovely brunette with dimples and deep blue eyes. They became engaged in June, and the wedding would be in October. One of the greatest delights of my life came when she agreed that I could make her wedding dress.

What a beautiful bride she was; in traditional white, with three attendants. Bev chose and bought the material and I made all the outfits. It was a work of love. The next best thing to having a daughter of my own!

Chapter Twenty-three
IMPROVEMENTS ON CANAL

Now that actual work had started on the St. Lawrence Seaway, we noticed many changes taking place on the Welland Canal. Improvements were being made at our lighthouse station as well, for this harbour, at the entrance to the canal, would be of vital importance in the years ahead.

Two new radio beacons were installed. These were of the latest design, and were synchronized to a new foghorn.

A concrete building was erected on the west pierhead, and a tower built on top housed a revolving light flashing red and white to be used as an aircraft beacon as well as a pierhead marker. A high steel tower was build adjacent to the radio building for a new antenna for the beacons.

The old acetylene pierhead lights were replaced by the latest type flashing lights which came on automatically when the sun went down or when visibility dropped, due to fog or storm. All aids to navigation, with the exception of these two pierhead lights, were remotely controlled from a panel of switches in the Watchroom.

Our canal road was suddenly alive with hundreds of workmen. First came surveyors and planners, and dozens of officials; then men in small boats testing the depth of the harbour, every inch of the way. Wherever it was found necessary to deepen the waterway, pumping equipment was utilized. Workmen toiled through all kinds of weather, day and night, with dredges, which sucked up earth and rocks from the bottom of the canal. This was carried across the road through a huge tube-like conveyor which continued on across the pier, spewing its contents into the lake. This process went on continuously day and night for several months.

The heavy equipment and trucks made a terrible mess of our poor old dirt road, and it was almost worth one's life to travel down it.

A level of 27 feet was to be maintained throughout the entire chain of waterways. Originally, the Welland Canal had been 27 feet deep but over the years parts of it had filled in to a shallower depth.

The canal proper, between the locks, was drained of water the moment navigation ended each season. Hundreds of bulldozers, trucks and diggers worked unceasingly throughout the winter months, deepening and widening the floor of the canal. The surrounding area was a beehive of activity.

Once it became known that construction had actually started on the Seaway, hundreds of canal watchers arrived daily, armed with cameras, binoculars, drawing boards, and a burning desire to get close to the ships as they sailed along the waterway.

Many planned their holidays to include a side trip to see the canal, for they had heard it was a new and exciting place to visit. They were amazed to learn that ocean ships had used the waterway for many years.

Distinguished visitors from distant countries toured the entire length of the canal, marvelling at the size of the locks and the mountainous height the ships had to climb from one lake level to the other. The twin locks at Thorold intrigued thousands of people who were viewing the canal for the first time.

We too had our share of visitors from far-away places: Bernard Harrison, the United Kingdom Trade Commissioner in Hong Kong; Dr. Rodgers, a well-known heart specialist from Burbank, California and his wife, a former Superintendent of Nurses at UCLA; Boy Scouts from many countries who were attending a Boy Scout Jambouree at Niagara-on-the-Lake; and Noel and Martha Edwards of the American State Department.

Cy and I took great pride in showing off our lighthouse, the canal operations and our radio shack, and our guests were charmed by everything they saw.

It was remarkable how the Edwards came to call on us. During the winter when Cy and I were in California, we visited a ham friend in Santa Monica. During the evening he began taping a message to send to some friends in Beirut, Lebanon. He asked us to say a few words into the microphone; tell them who we were, and about our home in Canada. I said:

"This is Ethel Williamson, VE3DTW, I live at a lighthouse on the Welland Canal, just fifteen miles from Niagara Falls. If you ever get a chance to visit the Falls, remember that we live very near, and we would love to see you."

Well, about three months later, I answered a knock on the front door. There stood a handsome young couple of strangers. I was greeted by a cheery "Hello!" then, "How would you like some visitors from Beirut, Lebanon? We're Noel and Martha Edwards, and we just couldn't resist your invitation to call!"

For a moment I was stunned. I had never expected to see these people; never thinking for a moment they would take me seriously; but here they were, in the flesh. I recovered my composure and, hoping to correct any impression of reluctance, I warmly invited them to come right in.

The outcome was a delightful day-long visit with two of the most interesting people Cy and I have ever met. Conditions in Beirut at that time were in a chaotic state, and they had been through some hectic happenings. Noel had a new car waiting for them in New York on their arrival from overseas. They decided to drive home to California, but to see Niagara Falls first. This led them to visit us.

The many guests whom we had during the summer that year helped us to eat up all the fish Cy had cleaned and put into the freezer compartment of our refrigerator. The silver bass were running that year. Hundreds of fishermen swarmed over the canal banks. We had so many fish fries that summer we finally became sick of them.

Some of our visitors were people with whom Cy and I had stayed during our trip to Europe. Ron Plant, G5CP, who had arranged for my British broadcast, was one of them. An electrical engineer, he stopped off here, on his return trip to England from a business trip to St. Louis, Missouri. Frank and Jessie MacAinsh, of Crieff, Scotland, were very welcome guests, too. They had just completed a tour of the United States, from Maine to California, where they visited our mutual friend, Maxine. The first thing they did, on arriving at the lighthouse, was to don their swim suits for a dip in the Welland Canal. "I've carried this swim suit around for two months," said Jessie, "and this is the first opportunity I've had to use it." Later, at dinner, she was worried about her hair.

"We're invited to a party at the Royal York tomorrow night," she said, and my hair looks awful after my swim."

"I can take care of that, Jessie," I told her. "You see, I used to be a hairdresser!" She was delighted at the news.

I was very pleased when Evelyn Scott, W6NZP, came to visit us from Long Beach, California. We had been radio friends for a long time, and I had met her a number of times in California.

Evelyn and her late husband were world travellers who had circled the globe three times, but they had never been to Canada. As this had been a long-planned trip, Evelyn decided to make the journey alone. By train and bus she had gone north as far as the Yukon; had crossed western Canada, and had spent two weeks at Churchill. By the time she arrived at our house she was completely exhausted. I urged her to rest for a few days but she was determined to see everything.

Knowing how thrilled Maxine had been with our sightseeing ride along the Niagara River, I decided to take Evelyn along the same route. What a ride! No sooner had we started out than Evelyn fell asleep. "Don't let me miss a thing," she had begged me, but I didn't have the heart to keep wakening her.

Finally, arriving at the aerial ride over the Niagara Gorge, I parked the car and gently told her where we were.

Springing into action, she jumped from the car and began pulling my arm. "Come," she insisted, "we must go for a ride."

"Not I," I said. "Why, I've never dreamed of going."

"Well, then, I'm going alone," she declared. Well, she was my guest; I couldn't allow that, so, reluctantly, and quite terrified, I went with her; saying a silent prayer all the time.

"Now," cried Evelyn, "I've ridden on every aerial ride in the world!"

A most unusual guest was Fred Carter, from Fiji.

Fred was in charge of the Beachcomber Hotel in Fiji, and a well-known radio ham. He had travelled to American Samoa, Hawaii, and Los Angeles before coming to Canada, taking about a month to get here. His destination was his family home in England, and he would spend about one week with us at the lighthouse.

Fred was a good-looking, affable bachelor, and a pleasant chap to have around, but when he arrived he had a problem.

"I've lost my tan!" he bewailed. "After being copper coloured for fifteen years, I can't face my people in England looking like this. They'll think I've been telling lies about my glorious tan." He glanced up and down the pier, then said, "Why, this is a perfect place. I can sun bathe right here."

"In the nude?" I asked, startled. Then I added, "You can't do that around here."

Cy broke into the conversation at this point. "You can climb up on the parapet roof," he said. "No one can see you from there."

Fred was suddenly aglow with anticipation. "That's a wonderful idea!" he declared, and from that day until the end of his stay he spent at least six hours each day lying on the lighthouse roof. He regained the tan, and flew to England confident that he would astound his people with his startling blue eyes and his bronze complexion.

One day a special delivery letter arrived from Maxine in California. "Please be on the air this Friday at 6 PM your time," she wrote. "Prince Talal and Princess Muna of Saudi Arabia will be my guests for lunch. We are old friends on radio, and he has heard me speak so often of you and Cy at the lighthouse, that he asked me to make a schedule with you for a chat over my station. He is travelling incognito, and I can't tell anyone around here of his visit until he leaves."

This was exciting news, and we were ready and waiting at the appointed time. At last it was 6 o'clock. Maxine introduced them as Talal and Muna. They were a charming couple, who spoke excellent English. We chatted for nearly an hour. Talal told us they were hoping to find time in their itinerary to visit Niagara Falls. "If we can make it, may we call on you at your lighthouse?" he asked. We assured him we would be very pleased to see them. For the next week or so I lived in expectation of their visit, then I heard from Maxine over radio that they had been obliged to return to Saudi Arabia, sooner than expected. Although they didn't come to the lighthouse, I was delighted to know they had wanted to come.

Maxine told me later that Princess Muna was beautiful as well as young and charming, and she wore a Christian Dior sundress. Prince Talal, who has since been featured in Life Magazine, was very democratic, and was in favour of drastic reforms in his country. His brother, Faisal, did not agree with Talal's policies, so Talal left the country.

Chapter Twenty-four
SEAWAY MANIA

The winter of 1958 brought a feverish last-minute rush of work on the canal. The St. Lawrence Seaway was scheduled to open the next spring and everything must be in readiness.

The Port Weller Drydocks nearby were very busy too. They had purchased the Muir Drydocks at Port Dalhousie and this gave them additional facilities for the building and repairing of ships. Their newest steamship, "Seaway Queen," was ready to sail the lakes. Everyone felt the excitement mounting. Would the Seaway be ready in time?

Cy now had a number of new tasks to perform since modernization was the order of the day. A hydrographical study of water levels on the Great Lakes and rivers was a daily duty. Many tiny buildings containing measuring devices were built in all strategic areas. One was erected on the lake side of our pier. A weekly report must be sent to Ottawa on the same day, on the same hour, from each station, assuring that all reports arrive at the main office at the same time for the scientific study of the over-all picture.

Another thing that must be very accurate is the constant check of time signals from the Dominion Observatory Radio Station, CHU, Ottawa. The radio beacon signals must be accurate within one second of the correct time, otherwise one station's signals would overlap another's located in various ports on Lake Ontario. This would cause the same kind of interference one often hears on regular radio sets, and create a confusion of signals over the air. As the ships depend on these characteristic signals for their direction and position on the lake, it is most important that they be exact.

One evening, while taking his regular time check, Cy noticed something most unusual. He immediately notified CHU in Ottawa, and was very pleased, when, about a week later, he received a special acknowledgment from that department thanking him for his report on "The Day That Canada Was One Minute Slow!"

One Sunday evening I turned on the shortwave radio for my regular chat with Maxine, in California.

"Oh, Ethel," she began, excitedly, "I've just seen a special program on television; Dave Garroway's Wide Wide World. It was all about the progess in the building of the St. Lawrence Seaway!"

"Isn't that nice," I said. "Cy and I were watching the same program. It was really wonderful to us, for although thisconstructionis going on all around us, we had no idea of the enormity of the project until we saw the actual work on TV. Just think, whole communities had to be re-located, where it was found necessary to cut a channel through a specific area!"

Lake Ontario

LIGHTHOUSE

EAST PIER

PORT WELLER HARBOUR

WIER!

CONTROL

SWING BRIDGE

DRYDOCKS

SHIPYARDS

Welland Ship Canal

TIEUP WALLS

PORT WELLER

LAKESHORE ROAD

ARN LANDS

AIR VIEW OF PORT WELLER HARBOUR, TAKEN IN 1959

"My biggest thrill was to see pictures of the Welland Canal. How it reminded me of the pleasant times we have spent together!"

For many months now we were to live in the midst of unexpected happenings. Time after time came officials of various branches of the government, touring the canal, looking at the progress of construction, and adding prestige and interest to this vast endeavour, with their comments and observations which were broadcast in every news media.

Senior Editors from such prominent magazines as National Geographic and US News and World Report were most anxious to hear our private views on the Seaway Project. I was thrilled to meet such distinguished men in person, but at that time we little realized the important role we would play with the opening of the Seaway.

Seaway Queen almost ready for opening of the Seaway 1959.

Chapter Twenty-five
THE SEAWAY OPENS!

No one could have foretold the incredible chain of events which accompanied the actual opening of the St. Lawrence Seaway.

Our lighthouse was well prepared for the opening of navigation, the first week of April, 1959. All lights were checked, radio equipment tested, reflectors re-silvered, foghorn synchronized, and all buildings freshly painted.

The canal opened on schedule, and regular freighters began sailing up and down the canal as they had done for years. The Seaway Queen, built within sight of our lighthouse, had her trial run on Lake Ontario. All that remained was the formal opening of the Seaway.

Our lightship tender, "The Grenville," a tough, black-hulled ship claimed the honour of being "First Ship" through the Seaway, even before this waterway opened the shipping route into the Great Lakes, for the 160-foot vessel went through the Iroquois Lock in November, 1958, officially opening the mile-long canal.

The "Grenville," a government-owned ship, besides carrying supplies to many lighthouses on Lake Ontario and Lake Erie, also built and repaired lighthouses. In addition to this, she was the foster-mother to a 206-buoy family in the St. Lawrence River. Her major task, just prior to the opening of the Seaway, was the placing of battery-operated lights to mark the new channel into the U.S. locks. Seventy light buoys mark the Canadian part of the channel. The United States Coast Guard cutter, "Maple," took care of the fifty buoys on the American side of the International Rapids.

Finally, traffic began speeding up on the Welland Canal. Any day now, we thought, the salties will be sailing by. How wrong we were! Due to heavy ice conditions at the entrance to the St. Lawrence River, the opening of the Port of Montreal, normally on the 15th of April, was delayed for ten days. By this time, an unprecedented number of foreign ships had arrived; each captain hoping to be the one having the honour to be the first to sail through the Seaway. In all, about 130 vessels, including tramp streamers, and brand new ships specially built for this new waterway, had arrived for the opening. When this actually came on April 25th, 1959, it created one of the worst traffic jams ever recorded.

Two days after the Seaway opened came the invasion of the Welland Canal.

On Sunday afternoon, April 26, the Dutch motorship, Prins Johan Willem Frisco, passed its sister ship, Prins Willem George Frederik, off Kingston, to become the first Seaway-borne ship to enter Lake Ontario. It entered Port Weller Harbour about 2:45 a.m. the next day, being the first foreign vessel to proceed through the Seaway. Its passing through the Welland Canal, in the dead of night, was uneventful and unannounced. It made its way up the lakes to Milwaukee and Chicago — another first, where it was greeted by helicopters, dropping flowers, fire-tugs spouting streams of water into the air, factory whistles, church bells and a civic reception. This was the harbinger of wonderful things to come for the ports-of-call, for millions of people and for our two great countries.

"Britannia".

Ships began racing for the Welland Canal. They were arriving every few minutes, each one hoping to proceed immediately through the canal. This was only one of the mistaken ideas, for it takes approximately eight hours to lock a vessel from one lake to the other. In the first twenty-four hour period, 21 ships were locked through Lock 1, upbound; 18 downbound. The downbound ships, going on their way from the upper Great Lakes, were our regular lake freighters, carrying out their normal shipping activities. By this time more than forty ships were at anchor off the Port Weller Harbour, awaiting entrance to the canal.

It was impossible to operate on the "first-come-first-served" principle, for the smaller vessels could go through the locks two at a time. When this procedure was observed, larger ships had to wait. The regulars were more adept at maneuvering through the locks on their own, but the newcomers found it difficult.

Pilots had to be rushed into service to guide them; their equipment was inadequate, and often useless, and in many cases their tie-up ropes were too short to reach the lock walls. It was a nightmare for the men delegated to help them through the canal.

Many of the captains had never sailed through a canal under their own steam. They were afraid, nervous and jittery. It was only natural. Some of them ran into lock walls, causing damage to the walls and their ships. Others waited hours longer than necessary, getting up enough courage to sail through without a tow. Nothing like this had ever happened before.

Amidst all this confusion, the canal broke down! Now the ships really piled up, for none was able to go through. News of this calamity was of international importance. Hordes of reporters, photographers and analysts descended on the lighthouse to see at first hand, and to report their findings.

There was nothing we could tell them, for we were kept too busy just tending to our own jobs. Finally, in desperation, we had to lock our gates to keep out the hundreds of curious who swarmed all over the pier. Still they came. It was a seven-day wonder that, somehow, never ended. So besieged were we by visitors, that it was necessary to have guards posted to keep the people out. Our chief concern was for the valuable radio equipment, housed at the west pierhead. It was impossible to keep constant watch on these outlying buildings and do our other work as well. Cy even had to replace pierhead lights a number of times, that had been deliberately shot out — for a lark!

"Thank God!" exclaimed Cy, when he saw the first Mountie arrive at the lighthouse. "I don't think we could have coped with this situation another day."

"I know you all want to see the ships," I had to tell people who called on the phone, hoping to wheedle their way past the guards, "but we have a tremendous job on our hands. No one must come down the pier unless on official business."

The East Pier was opened by the canal authorities, to the public. Cars were allowed to drive to the pierhead, where the occupants could look, take pictures, and wave to ships.

American Naval Ship in Lock I and Taylor's Refreshment Stand—serving sailors of the world.

1st Italian Ship to sail through Canal.

What an amazing sight this was from our lighthouse! Thousands of cars travelling at a snail's pace, bumper to bumper, all the way down to the end; then back, looking, from our vantage point, like a giant, moving chain.

The responsibility was tremendous. Every night I'd pray, "Please, God, don't let anything happen to the ships." Each morning, I'd thank God that all was well.

As many as fifty ships were in view, every day, for weeks. Ships of many nations, as far as one could see on the horizon. It looked like fairyland at night, with myriads of lights, but, in fact, it was a nightmare.

Early on Tuesday morning, May 7th, a dense fog descended, enveloping the ships like a smokescreen. This brought a new and terrifying danger. It grew thicker and thicker, creeping along the entire canal. Every ship on or near the waterway had to drop anchor; everything was paralyzed. The captains of the ships could do nothing but wait and fume.

We now had to double our vigilance every minute of each day, for the aids to navigation were not infallible. Even when there were a few minutes to sleep, it was almost impossible for the noises all around us. Every one of those fifty-odd ships blew fog signals to denote their position on the lake. Each whistle seemed to have a different tone. Port Dalhousie foghorn and ours seemed to be in competition for the louder; sometimes blowing alternately; sometimes in unison. This fog spell lasted about three days; then what a mad rush there was to get through the canal!

There would be a period of great activity and movement; then a breakdown or an accident on the canal, caused by a ship running into a wall or bridge; another frantic rush of shipping, and another heavy fog. And so it went on, never lessening the number of waiting ships, for the ones that sailed through the canal were immediately replaced by new arrivals from Montreal.

Then came the formal opening of the Seaway by Queen Elizabeth and President Eisenhower, on a lovely day, June 26, 1959.

We watched the proceedings on television, and Cy took photographs of the ceremonies, with his camera set in front of the television screen.

Any day now we could expect to see Her Majesty's ship, Britannia, sail through the canal. The Queen would not be aboard, but the ship was so well-known that its passage through the waterway would attract thousands of spectators.

Another scheduled event would be the arrival of a flotilla of American warships, which would pass through the Seaway from the Atlantic Ocean.

A few days after the formal opening of the Seaway, the fog was so thick it was impossible to see any of the ships at anchor, and traffic had been halted on the canal. Hearing a car horn blow outside, I ran to look out the kitchen window.

"Come quickly," I called to Cy. "There are two station wagons outside, filled with American naval officers!" We ran out to greet them.

One officer, the spokesman for the group, introduced himself and said, "We're the official welcoming party for the American warships. Three of the ships are lying at anchor just outside the entrance to the canal. They were due to arrive in Buffalo this morning, but, owing to the tie-up of shipping, they

Fort York - C.S.L. - in Lock I
on her maiden voyage.

can't make it. The ships' officers were scheduled to describe their first voyage through the Seaway on a radio programme. We've been talking to them on ship-to-shore telephone, and they will make a tape recording of their impressions, to be broadcast later in the day. They're sending a launch to take us out to the ships. Have we permission to use your dock?"

"It's our pleasure," Cy told him. We were both thinking of all the times our little dock had proven its worth over the years. From now on it would have more use than ever.

The officers parked the station wagons and stood chatting with us until a motor launch appeared, heading towards the lighthouse. Six sailors stood stiffly at attention, although the boat was bobbing up and down as it ploughed through the water.

The welcoming party climbed into the boat and it set out through the fog to return to the Oglethorpe, the lead ship of the flotilla.

After that, many senior officials arrived at the lighthouse, to be taken out to the various ships at anchor.

As soon as this lenghty spell of fog had lifted, ships sailed by in a steady stream. Freighters from Liberia, Italy, Greece, Israel and Spain, and much larger ships than ever before from England, The Netherlands, Scandinavian countries and West Germany; and others too numerous to mention.

Then came Dominion Day, and we were ready to greet the Britannia. Only members of our family and a few friends were permitted to pass through the gates to the lighthouse. They were warned to be inside the gates before eight o'clock.

What a beautiful clear day it was. The time for Britannia's arrival had been announced, and she would be given precedence over all ships on the lake, to enter the canal.

Long before she appeared on the horizon, we were ready, with cameras, flags and binoculars.

"Here she comes!" yelled Bruce, and he pointed to the west.

At first she was just a speck on the horizon, then, as she sailed towards us, we could see the huge freighters separate, making a clear pathway for her. As she came closer, hundreds of little pleasure boats trailed behind.

The yacht was an unassuming ship, but the whole panoramic scene before us was laid out like a super-colossal movie set. The sleek, navy blue vessel, with the air of a queen attended by her handmaidens, sailed majestically past the Titans of many nations, with little boats trailing like a bride's train. A lump came into my throat as she entered the harbour. Sailors in white stood shoulder to shoulder along her deck. I was so mesmerized by the sight, I almost forgot my cameras, for, as she sailed past the pierhead, I could have reached out and touched her side. Navy helicopters droned overhead, keeping guard, and the little boats followed her into the canal.

I suddenly remembered an old song my mother used to sing when I was a little girl. It was written for Queen Victoria, but somehow it seemed to fit this occasion, and this moment. As I recall, it went like this:

BRITANNIA

The ship that belongs to a lady
Has a good captain and crew.
When out on a trip on that beautiful ship
She's flying the red, white and blue.
The foreign ships treat her politely;
Her colours are pretty well known.
And because she belongs to a lady,
I reckon they'll leave her alone.

I was armed with two cameras; one, a movie camera, and the other for coloured slides. What a mad scramble, to make sure I had pictures on both of them!

Our cars were already turned, facing the lighthouse, for a quick dash back, to take more photos as the ship sailed past our house. My brother, James, stood, ready to lower our flag in salute. What a thrill, when we saw one of her sailors run to lower the ship's flag in answer!

The gates of Lock 1 had been opened, ready to receive the Britannia, and the lock walls, above, were lined with officials. As she sailed along the Welland Canal, she was cheered by holiday crowds in the thousands, who lined both sides of the canal, every inch of the way.

After the Britannia had passed through the canal, the weather remained fine for several days, and we were delighted to see more American warships, submarines, and the beauty of them all, the flagship, Macon. Once again, spectators came in thousands to watch and applaud. All this was reported in the news media all over the world. Where else, but on the Welland Canal could one see and almost touch ships from so many countries? Many people chatted with the sailors, mailed letters for them, and received souvenirs in return. Tourists came from every province in Canada, and from every state in the United States. Canal-watching became the exciting thing to do on one's holidays; for here, in the heart of a continent were ships and sailors from strange and distant lands.

S.S. J.N. McWatters.
Scott Misener Steamships.

A submarine

tied-up below Lock I.

III

Chapter Twenty-six
THE WELLAND CANAL AND THE SEAWAY

Since the opening of the Seaway in 1959, improvements on the Welland Canal have been fantastic. The increase in shipping has gone beyond all expectations and the future looks even brighter.

Many essential services are provided for ships and their crews, as they sail through the canal. When a ship arrives at the 2½-mile buoy, just north of the canal entrance, it is advised by radio telephone of the order of its passage through the canal; about wind conditions or any obstructions. The radio control centre at Thorold has a model of the canal with midget ships placed in position according to their movements. Closed-circuit television, a recently acquired aid to navigation, has greatly facilitated the movement of ships through the waterway.

Pilots had been used from the earliest days of sailing on the Great Lakes. These men, skilled in every aspect of sailing, would be taken aboard ship at one port; guide the ship through dangerous waters, then return to home port on another ship, sailing in that direction. Pilots, guiding ships through the Welland Canal would be taken aboard at Kingston, Ontario, then leave the ship at Sarnia. Just before the Seaway opened, it was customary for captains to sail in the Port Weller Harbour, and tie-up below Lock 1. There, a pilot would climb aboard, and take the ship through the canal.

It was only the foreign ships that required a pilot to guide them through the waterway, for captains of the lakers had had many years of sailing through the canal on their own.

With the opening of the Seaway, the Department of Transport sent a pilot boat to Port Weller with a complement of 18 trained pilots, to guide the ships through the Welland Canal. These men, former Lake sailors with Master Mariner's papers, were familiar with every hazard, every turn and twist in the canal.

By May 1, 1959, another pilot boat, the Qu'Appelle, designed by Captain G. G. Leask of the Department of Transport and Captain L. H. Crawford of St. Catharines, was brought to Port Weller to carry the pilots back and forth between the ships they were guiding through the canal. Before that navigation season was over, there were 45 qualified pilots on the Welland Canal!

The pilots were dispatched by ship-to-shore messages, from a pilotage office on the mainland. These men, carried in the little pilot boat, would approach the ship just outside the Port Weller Harbour. A ladder would be lowered from the big ship, and while the little boat maneuvered alongside, the pilot would climb the ladder to the deck of the ship. A special flag was then raised denoting the presence of a pilot aboard, and the ship would proceed under its own steam, through the waterway. The same procedure was used in going up the canal as in coming down to Lake Ontario. These pilots are on call twenty four hours each day; always in contact by ship-to-shore telephone communication with the pilotage office.

Frank Sherman.
Upper Lakes Shipping—taken prior to her
Christening.

Many times in rough weather I have prayed for the safety of these pilots, for it is no mean feat leaving a wee boat, tossing in the heavy seas like a plastic ball, to climb a flimsy rope ladder up the slippery wet side of a rolling ship. Sometimes it is only after several attempts that a pilot is safely aboard. In the early spring and fall, with the added danger of icing, it is even more dangerous. I often watch them, through binoculars, until I'm sure they are all right.

The seaway brought other problems to even the most skilful of pilots. Some foreign ships had draughts of 35-ft. Others had super-structures that interfered with the bridges over the canal. These high-riding ships were clumsy to handle in the canal in high winds, especially when travelling light, without cargo.

Some had flaring, wide-spreading bows for cutting through ocean waves; no protective bumpers at the sides; and tie-up ropes that were too short. All these problems have now been eliminated.

When a pilot is given a radio message to enter the canal, he guides the ship to the mooring wall below Lock 1. Here, men are lowered in a chair, by a long arm which swings them over the ship's side to the lock wall. Ropes or chains are thrown down to them, and the men fasten them securely to the bollards, where they remain until the message comes to enter the lock from a panel of coloured light flash signals, readily understood by the pilots.

From the moment the ship enters the lock until it leaves, the Lock Master, from his observation post above, controls the ship movements by loud speaker. This is often a tricky business, for many ships are 70 ft. wide and 800 ft. long. These must be carefully guided under their own power into locks 80 ft. wide and 820 ft. long. Smaller ships are often locked through several at a time. Canal linesmen, well-trained in their jobs, handle the ropes and the tying-up of all ships in the locks.

As a ship is being raised or lowered to lock wall level, sailors scramble down ladders at the side, making a bee-line for the refreshment stand, where they can buy cigarettes, magazines, camera film, soft drinks and other items. As the men have only about ten minutes before returning to the ship, you can well imagine the mad rush that ensues, trying to serve them in time.

Through the radio-telephone system, ships can order grocery supplies from marine stores that have serviced the ships for many years. Local dairies are also on the alert for calls, twenty-four hours each day, to supply milk, butter and eggs to the ships.

Bags of laundry and dry-cleaning are taken off the ships at either end of the canal, to be returned at the other end after the passage through the canal.

Ship repairs are done at the shipyards above Lock 1, and garbage is removed at special stops. Although it is frowned on, clothing salesmen manage to get aboard the ships to take measurements for suits, to be delivered on the return trip.

Many silent services are given to the crews of ships in the canal. The most important, I believe, is a visit of the canal Chaplain. In the past one hundred years there have been just three Chaplains on the Welland Ship Canals. These missions, which were started by the Reverend Bone (called Father Bone by the sailors) are inter-denominational. Father Bone served as Canal Chaplain for thirty-eight years. The Reverend James Judson then took over the mission, serving for thirty-six years. The present Chaplain, Reverend Cameron Orr, has looked after the sailors' spiritual needs for over twenty-five years. This has been an arduous but rewarding work.

S.S. Gleneagles–Canada Steamship Lines.

"Many times," says Mr. Orr, "I've been ordered to leave a ship; sometimes followed by jeering sailors; often by curses. Most captains are receptive and happy to have a minister aboard, even though it's only for an hour. I confine my activities to the area of the Flight Locks. It takes a ship just about an hour to go up or down, and I must complete my work in that time."

Reception from foreign ships has been tremendous, for Mr. Orr carries the Gospel, written in many languages, and there are ships from more than thirty countries using this waterway. One Greek ship gave him an exceptionally warm welcome. "Papa, you come again!" the men called, when he had to leave the ship.

A British captain told him, "You are the first Padre to say prayers on my ship in forty years!"

"These men are without religion for ten months of each year," says Mr. Orr. "They have many problems, and I'm here to help them. I have many sailors call at our home on their free time, and have arranged their weddings in my living room."

One of the most interesting things about canal watching is the display of flags on the ships. The flag denoting the country in which the ship is registered is flown at the stern. Other flags, such as company flags, and that of Canada, (when sailing in Canadian waters) and various others are flown from the main mast. A red flag, denoting oil barges and gasoline carriers is displayed prominently on these ships, and a special pilot's flag is flown to denote a pilot is aboard.

Prominently displayed on the smokestacks are the colourful and sometimes garish insignia of the various ships' companies or owners. Crowns, stars, animals and birds are familiar symbols. Some companies use large letters of the alphabet; others are most unique.

One day, one of our grandsons, watching a large ship from Belfast, Ireland, sail past the lighthouse, questioned Cy. "Grandpa," he asked, "why is this ship called the 'Head line,' when the picture on the smokestack is a big red hand?"

"It's a very old story," Cy explained. "The Red Hand is the ancient symbol of the Kingdom of Ulster. Tradition has it that in the pre-Christian era of Ireland, when the country was divided into four kingdoms, the throne of Ulster was left vacant. The king of Leinster (who was the senior monarch) had the right to decide the succession. But he also had two sons, each of whom claimed right to the throne. It was decided to settle the issue by having a long-boat race up the coast from Leinster, and the first one to touch Ulster soil would be declared the winner.

"The race between the brothers brought forth a dazzling and cunning display of seamanship, but as the long-boats approached the quay of the harbour, it became apparent the race would end in a tie. Red Hugh O'Neil, one of the two, drew his sword — severed his left hand at the wrist, and threw it ashore!"

"Wow! Grandpa. That was an awful thing to do."

"Well, Brucie, some men will do anything to win. When he threw his hand ashore, he fulfilled the requirement of being the first to touch the soil of Ulster, and was declared the winner, thus becoming the King of Ulster. The Red Hand, with three drops of blood at the wrist, has become the symbol of the country of Northern Ireland, as it is currently constituted, and is used by the Head Lines to signify the nationality of their ships."

"Oh, I see. Just like some of our ships use the Maple Leaf."

"That's right." Cy knocked the dead ash from his pipe, put in some fresh tobacco, and re-lighted it. After taking a couple of deep draws on it, he said, "Y'know something, Brucie, I bet there's a story behind most of the symbols on smokestacks but I'm sure there are none as exciting as the one about the Red Hand."

"You're right, Popeye," Brucie agreed, a wide smile lighting his face. Popeye was the grandchildren's favourite nickname for Cy, and when grandpa told them a story it was a special occasion. They just loved it.

Ulster
Steamship Co., Ltd.
Belfast, Ireland

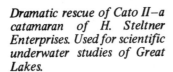

S.S. Thorold of the Ontario Paper Co. fleet carrying pulpwood to the mill—this traffic has been in operation since 1913.

Dramatic rescue of Cato II—a catamaran of H. Steltner Enterprises. Used for scientific underwater studies of Great Lakes.

Chapter Twenty-seven
THE SALTIES DASH TO THE SEA

Every year nearing the closing of the navigation season there is a mad scramble to clear the inland waterways of ships before they are "iced in" for the winter.

The captains, too, are anxious to complete their final trip of the year before the insurance rates are increased, due to additional hazards with bad weather conditions. At the same time, they often take a chance on one more voyage and one final cargo. This can be disastrous.

The worst situation I recall came early in November, 1965. "FIFTY SHIPS AT ANCHOR OFF PORT WELLER!" was top news of that day.

After the most successful year on the Seaway, this had to happen!

Most of the vessels, riding out the gale-force winds in the harbour were lakers. They still had plenty of time to make their final upbound passage before the navigation season ended. It was the salties that were in for real trouble. This would be their last trip to the upper lakes with cargoes from abroad. Most of them would then fill their holds with precious wheat and other vital goods to take back across the Atlantic.

All shipping had been advised, well in advance, of the closing dates in various parts of the Seaway. Port Arthur, Fort William and Duluth close early. The locks at Sault St. Marie are the first to close in the winter. The Port of Montreal has a deadline of December 3rd. This is usually the final date for ocean vessels in the St. Lawrence Seaway. Port Weller closes on December 15th, the same date as the Welland Canal.

All captains are well aware of these closing dates, and most of them plan their trips to be well away before these deadlines. Some, however, take a chance on one more passage through the Seaway, only to be caught in ice. This means spending the three winter months at a Canadian or American port.

This is a dangerous and expensive piece of business. The holds are filled with valuable cargo, and many of the sailors must be flown back to their homelands, leaving a skeleton crew to guard the ship.

In 1964, four foreign ships were stranded this way. Now, once again we were faced with hundreds of ships unable to proceed through the canal due to weather conditions.

After a closedown of 28½ hours, ships began moving through the canal. All masters of ocean ships were again warned of the closing deadlines. The skippers were asked to adjust their schedule to prevent being trapped by ice.